DK EYEWITNESS

T0063621

TOP **10**
ICELAND

Top 10 Iceland Highlights

Welcome to Iceland **5**

Exploring Iceland **6**

Iceland Highlights **10**

Þingvellir National Park **12**

The Blue Lagoon and Around **14**

Geysir Hot Springs Area **16**

Gullfoss...**18**

Lake Mývatn Area **20**

Vatnajökull National Park **24**

Snæfellsjökull National Park......**26**

Látrabjarg Bird Cliffs **28**

Landmannalaugar Area **30**

Jökulsárlón **32**

The Top 10 of Everything

Moments in History **36**

Churches **38**

Museums in Reykjavík..................**40**

Museums Around Iceland **42**

Waterfalls **44**

Volcanoes.....................................**46**

Hot Springs and Geysers.............**48**

Places to See Birds
and Wildlife **50**

Outdoor Activities........................**52**

Hiking Trails **54**

Children's Activities.....................**58**

Nightlife **60**

Fine Dining Restaurants..............**62**

Cheaper Eats in Reykjavík...........**64**

Iceland for Free **66**

Festivals..**68**

Offshore Islands..........................**70**

CONTENTS

Iceland
Area by Area

Reykjavík.................................**74**

West Iceland and the
    Snæfellsnes Peninsula...........**82**

The Westfjords **88**

North Iceland **94**

East Iceland.................................**100**

South Iceland **108**

The Highland Interior **114**

Streetsmart

Getting Around **120**

Practical Information.................**122**

Places to Stay............................**128**

General Index.............................**134**

Acknowledgments.....................**140**

Phrase Book...............................**142**

Map Index....................................**144**

Within each Top 10 list in this book, no hierarchy
of quality or popularity is implied. All 10 are,
in the editor's opinion, of roughly equal merit.

Title page, front cover and spine *The aurora
borealis over Kirkjufell mountain and waterfall*
Back cover, clockwise from top left *Sunset
at Reykjavík harbour; snowboarding in Bláfjöll;
couple of puffins in the Westfjords; aurora
borealis at Kirkjufell; Reykjavík cityscape*

The rapid rate at which the world is changing
is constantly keeping the DK Eyewitness team
on our toes. While we've worked hard to
ensure that this edition of Iceland is accurate
and up-to-date, we know that opening hours
alter, standards shift, prices fluctuate, places
close and new ones pop up in their stead. So,
if you notice we've got something wrong or
left something out, we want to hear about it.
Please get in touch at **travelguides@dk.com**

Welcome to
Iceland

Famed for its wild natural beauty, Iceland enchants visitors with its thundering waterfalls, lunar-like lava deserts, smouldering volcanoes and majestic fjords. It also has a rich Viking heritage – many of the renowned sagas were written here – as well as a thriving contemporary culture. With DK Eyewitness Top 10 Iceland, it's yours to explore.

Here you can spend never-ending summer days strolling **Reykjavík's** historic centre, taking an outdoor thermal soak in the surreal waters of the **Blue Lagoon** or enjoying fresh-caught salmon or lobster in a seafront restaurant. Adventurous travellers can also tackle the **Laugavegur** trail between **Landmannalaugar's** hot springs and the beautiful highland wilderness at Þórsmörk, or gaze at powder-blue icebergs drifting lazily around at **Jökulsárlón**. It's all here on this island nation, floating just below the Arctic Circle.

It is not just the country's landscape that draws visitors here. Small but sophisticated Reykjavík offers a melange of cafés, bars and museums. Meanwhile, history and the elements are visibly entangled at sites such as **Þingvellir**, the rift-valley location of Iceland's original Viking parliament, and **Laxárdalur**, the setting for the tragic *Laxdæla Saga*. But in the end, it's Iceland's raw beauty that really captures the imagination: the smouldering lava fields, huge volcanic craters, bubbling mud pools and seething geysers.

Whether you're visiting for a weekend or a week, our Top 10 guide brings together the best of everything that Iceland has to offer, from four-wheel-drive expeditions across the Interior to gentle walks around Reykjavík's city parks. The guide has useful tips throughout, from seeking out what's free to the best outdoor activities, plus nine easy-to-follow itineraries, designed to tie together a clutch of sights in a short space of time. Add inspiring photography and detailed maps, and you've got the essential pocket-sized travel companion. **Enjoy the book, and enjoy Iceland**.

Clockwise from top: Jökulsárlón icebergs, the Blue Lagoon, Hallgrímskirkja in Reykjavík, Eyjafjallajökull volcano erupting, Vík church, a puffin, turf houses in Djúpivogur

Exploring Iceland

Iceland's attractions are split between its unique island culture and its spectacular scenery – and with many landscapes closely tied to famous historic events, you'll often find both together. Here are some ideas for making the most of your stay, whether you are here on a weekend break in Reykjavík, or have time to circuit the country.

Reykjavík's old house are weatherproofed in brightly coloured corrugated iron.

Strokkur geyser erupts every few minutes.

Key
— Two-day itinerary
— Seven-day itinerary

Two Days in Iceland

Day ❶
Stroll around Reykjavík's midtown and harbour (see p75), taking in the Harpa concert hall (see p76) and cultural exhibitions at Landnámssýningin, Safnahúsið and Listasafn Íslands (see p75). In the afternoon, survey the city from atop Hallgrímskirkja (see p76) or Perlan (see p77) before admiring Modernist canvases at Kjarvalsstaðir (see p76). End the day at Laugardalur Park (see p77) botanic gardens, appreciating the over 5,000 species of plants.

Day ❷
Take a Golden Circle tour (or drive) around the ancient parliament site at Þingvellir (see pp12–13), Geysir's hot pools and waterspouts (see pp16–17) and the thundering falls of Gullfoss (see pp18–19). Enjoy an evening soak at the Blue Lagoon (see pp14–15).

Seven Days in Iceland

Day ❶
Explore Reykjavík's historic midtown and harbour (see p75), taking in the excellent, subterranean Landnámssýningin exhibition (see p75). Drive around the iconic landscapes at Þingvellir (see pp12–13), Geysir (see pp16–17) and Gullfoss (see pp18–19), before heading past Kerið crater (see p112) to spend the night in the town of Selfoss.

Day ❷
Travel the southwest coast, via the Hvolsvöllur Saga Centre (see p112),

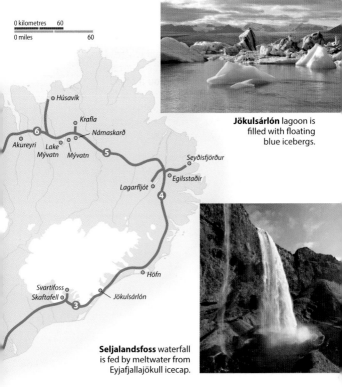

0 kilometres 60
0 miles 60

Húsavík

Krafla

Námaskarð

Akureyri Lake Mývatn
Mývatn

Seyðisfjörður

Egilsstaðir

Lagarfljót

Höfn

Svartifoss
Skaftafell

Jökulsárlón

Jökulsárlón lagoon is
filled with floating
blue icebergs.

Seljalandsfoss waterfall
is fed by meltwater from
Eyjafjallajökull icecap.

the waterfall at **Seljalandsfoss**
(see p44), the striking **Eyjafjallajökull**
icecap *(see p46)* – site of the 2010
eruption – and **Skógafoss** *(see p45)*.
Stay overnight at **Vík** *(see p110)*,
with its teeming seabird colonies.

Day ❸
Cross the gravel desert that lies
east of Vík to **Skaftafell** *(see p25)*,
where you can see glacier tongues
and the **Svartifoss** waterfall *(see
p54)*. Continue to the icebergs at
Jökulsárlón *(see pp32–3)* and lobster
restaurants at **Höfn** *(see p103)*,
with views of the **Vatnajökull**
icecap *(see p24)* along the way.

Day ❹
Travel up the east coast and then
inland to **Egilsstaðir** *(see p101)*,
where you could either circuit

Lagarfljót *(see p103)* or head to the
picturesque East Fjords port of
Seyðisfjörður *(see p102)*.

Day ❺
Drive towards **Lake Mývatn**
(see pp20–21), detouring to
explore the Krafla eruption site
and Námaskarð's mud pools.
Circuit Lake Mývatn before unwin-
ding at Mývatn Nature Baths.

Day ❻
Head to the north coast for a
whale-watching trip out of **Húsavík**
(see p96), before driving to pleasant
Akureyri *(see p96)*.

Day ❼
Return to Reykjavík and spend a
couple of hours at the **Blue Lagoon**
(see pp14–15) en route to the airport.

Top 10 Iceland Highlights

Jökulsárlón glacier lagoon at sunset

Iceland Highlights	10	Vatnajökull National Park	24
Þingvellir National Park	12	Snæfellsjökull National Park	26
The Blue Lagoon and Around	14	Látrabjarg Bird Cliffs	28
Geysir Hot Springs Area	16	Landmannalaugar Area	30
Gullfoss	18	Jökulsárlón	32
Lake Mývatn Area	20		

TOP 10 Iceland Highlights

Sitting on an active volcanic ridge at the edge of the Arctic Circle, Iceland is known for its landscapes: dramatic waterfalls, fiery volcanoes, spouting geysirs and windswept lava fields. The island also has a rich history, seen in its museums and historic sights, as well as a vibrant culture, encountered everywhere from tiny fishing villages to cosmopolitan Reykjavík.

Þingvellir National Park 1

This broad rift valley – which continues to expand thanks to still-shifting tectonic plates – was the site of Iceland's Viking parliament *(see pp12–13)*.

2 The Blue Lagoon

Take a sauna or soak in the pale blue waters of Iceland's most sublime outdoor spa set among black lava boulders *(see pp14–15)*.

3 Geysir Hot Springs Area

Just an hour from Reykjavík, this hillside of bubbling pools and erupting waterspouts has given its name to similar formations around the world *(see pp16–17)*.

Gullfoss 4

This powerful waterfall has been a national symbol since it was saved from oblivion during the 1920s *(see pp18–19)*.

5 Lake Mývatn Area

Lake Mývatn is home to the best of Iceland in one place: wildfowl, volcano cones, mud pits, steaming lava flows and thermal pools *(see pp20–21)*.

Ísafjörður
Gjögur
Þingeyri
Bíldudalur
Hólmavík
8
Látrabjarg Bird Cliffs
Brjánslækur
Breiðafjörður
Laugar
Ólafsvík
Stykkishólmur
Brú
7
Vegamót
Snæfellsjökull National Park
Bifröst
Borgarnes
Faxaflói
Gullfoss
Þingvellir National Park 1
3
Reykjavík
Geysir Hot Springs Area
The Blue Lagoon 2
Selfoss
Hvolsvöllur

6 Vatnajökull National Park

This reserve protects not only the Vatnajökull icecap and its out-running glaciers, but also beautiful rivers, gorges and mountain formations *(see pp24–5)*.

7 Snæfellsjökull National Park

Western Iceland's peninsula peaks with the snowy cone of Snæfellsjökull, a slumbering volcano crossed by hiking trails. It is tall enough to be visible from Reykjavík *(see pp26–7)*.

8 Látrabjarg Bird Cliffs

Fantastically remote even by Icelandic standards, north-westerly Látrabjarg supports one of the largest seabird colonies in Europe, and is home to millions of gulls, guillemots and puffins *(see pp28–9)*.

10 Jökulsárlón

Travel along the Ringroad to this lagoon between the Breiðamerkurjökull glacier and the Atlantic Ocean, which is full of seals and icebergs *(see pp32–3)*.

9 Landmannalaugar Area

Its bridgeless rivers, shattered grey mountains and hot springs make you feel like an explorer in the wild, but summer buses make this area easily accessible for visitors *(see pp30–31)*.

TOP 10 ⭐ Þingvellir National Park

Iceland's location on the mid-Atlantic ridge is obvious at Þingvellir (Assembly Plains), where the land has crashed in a deep scar stretching north from Lake Þingvallavatn. In AD 930, this dramatic setting was chosen by the island's chieftains as the site of their annual Alþing (General Assembly). Almost 4,000 of the country's roughly 40,000 inhabitants gathered here to hear laws and to settle disputes, occasionally by combat. The Alþing's power declined after Iceland accepted Norwegian sovereignty in 1262, but the assembly continued to be held here until 1798.

1 Lögberg

A prominent outcrop below Almannagjá's cliffs marks the site where the Alþing's Lawspeaker stood and recited the country's laws to the masses below. Look nearby for faint outlines of *buðir*, the tented camps used during Viking times.

2 Þingvellir Church

This surprisingly low-key wooden building with a black roof **(below)** is a reminder of the Alþing of AD 1000, when, despite strong opposition from pagan priests and chieftains, the Icelandic nation adopted Christianity as its sole religion under threat of Norwegian invasion *(see p36)*. The church was built in 1859 but it has a pulpit that dates back to 1683.

3 Volcanic Features

The broad, flattened dome of northerly Skjaldbreiður – an ancient shield volcano – was the source of the lava flow now covering Þingvellir's valley. Cut by deep fissures, the lava cooled into rough *a'a* outcrops and pavements of smoother *pahoehoe* (both of which are types of lava).

4 Almannagjá

A walk through Almannagjá's deep, cliff-lined gully **(above)** is a good way to appreciate Þingvellir's geology. Here, as the North American and European continental plates drift apart at a rate of 2.5 cm (1 inch) a year, Iceland is literally ripping in half.

5 Þingvallavatn

At 84 sq km (33 sq miles), Þingvallavatn **(below)** is the largest natural lake in Iceland. Its clear waters are famous for char and trout fishing, as well as scuba diving.

6 Flora

Þingvellir valley's floor is covered in a thick carpet of moss, lichen, orchids, dwarf willow and birch. Visit in autumn for exceptional colours and join the locals in picking crowberries **(left)**, which are used to make jam.

7 Öxarárfoss

Legend has it that the Öxaráfoss falls were created when the river was diverted in around AD 930 to provide drinking water during the assemblies. In medieval times, executions were carried out here.

8 Wildlife

The area just to the north of Þingvallavatn's lakeshore abounds in interesting wildlife. Keep an eye out for swans, mergansers **(right)** and northern divers on the water, as well as snipes, ptarmigans, minks and Arctic foxes on land.

9 Visitor Centre

Perched atop the western side of the rift, on Route 36, the Visitor Centre offers great views of Þingvellir. It's also home to the Heart of Iceland, an interactive exhibition where visitors can learn about the area.

10 Peningagjá

Peningagjá is an extraordinary sight: a narrow but deep lava fissure flooded with clear, peacock-blue water. At the bottom of this well you can see the glinting coins left by hopeful visitors.

PAYING THE PENALTY

Law courts at the Alþing strangely had no power to enforce their judgments. Litigants accepted the verdicts because they reflected public opinion, but in theory – and sometimes in practice – powerful men could ignore the sentences against them. The courts tried to resolve serious disputes through mediation, but some were sentenced to the highest Viking penalty: to be banished to the country's barren interior for 20 years and then killed.

NEED TO KNOW

MAP C5 ■ From Reykjavík, Golden Circle tour buses visit Þingvellir daily year-round; if driving, allow 60–90 minutes via Route 36; parking fee is ISK750 ■ Bus schedule: www.bsi.is ■ www.thingvellir.is/en

■ From the Visitor Centre, through the cliffs of Almannagjá, descend to the Law Rock. Take a detour to see the extraordinary Peningagjá and the church, then walk up to Öxarárfoss. In good weather, follow hiking tracks up the rift to see some abandoned farms, but take extra care as the dense undergrowth hides deep fissures.

■ The Visitor Centre near Hakið also has a souvenir shop and a small café.

TOP 10 ★ The Blue Lagoon and Around

The Blue Lagoon (*Bláa Lónið*) is Iceland's premier geothermal spa and one of the country's most beautiful. Set in a desolate lava wilderness, the lagoon's bright blue waters add a surreal splash of colour. You can laze in the steaming waters, have a beauty treatment, enjoy an excellent meal or stay nearby and catch the seasonal display of the aurora borealis. If you have your own transport, explore some of the unusual sights around the lagoons, including Grindavík's Saltfish Museum, the Seltún Hot Springs and Selatangar's abandoned fishing camp.

① Background and Origin

The tranquil Blue Lagoon was created when geothermal sea-water flowing out of the Svartsengi Geothermal Power Station collected in the surrounding lava **(above)**. Locals discovered that a warm dip cured skin ailments and public facilities opened here during the 1980s.

② Unique Lava Setting

The lagoon is bordered by rough masses of black lava boulders, which lie piled high around the perimeter, hemming in the powder-blue waters.

③ Geothermal Spa

The water, at a temperature of 37°C (99°F), is comfortable and the vast lagoon **(below)** is an amazing place to unwind, with an adjacent sauna.

④ Spa Services

Enjoy a relaxing massage in a private area of the lagoon itself **(above)**, or opt for a cleansing rub-down using the naturally processed fine silica, minerals, algae and salt distilled from the Blue Lagoon's waters. Beauty treatments are also available. It is a good idea to book any spa treatments in advance.

⑤ Dermatology and Health Clinics

The Blue Lagoon's mineral salts and silica have long enjoyed a repu-tation for quickly relieving eczema, psoriasis and other skin problems. You can seek specialized treatment while staying at the clinic near the lagoon or simply buy products that you can use at home.

⑥ Lava Restaurant

Enjoy Icelandic dishes, such as grilled lobster with garlic butter or fillet of lamb, with a view of the lagoon from your table. There's also an excellent bar accessible from the water and a café selling snacks.

GEOTHERMAL POWER

Svartsengi Geothermal Power Station takes advantage of its location over a fault line to give cheap, green power and hot water to the Reykjanes Peninsula. Geothermal seawater is pumped over 1 km (0.6 miles) underground, turns to steam and is used to drive the turbines that help produce 76 MW of electricity. The steam is then cooled and released into the Blue Lagoon. Five geothermal plants produce a quarter of the nation's electricity.

⑦ Icelandic Saltfish Museum

At Grindavík, a short drive south, is this eccentric museum **(left)** that traces the fishing heritage of Iceland through dioramas and photographs.

⑩ Overnight Stay

Accommodation options for overnight stay include The Retreat at Blue Lagoon *(see p129)*, Silica Hotel and the Northern Lights Inn. The latter is a fantastic spot during winters, when the colourful aurora borealis can at times be seen across the night sky.

⑧ Seltún Hot Springs

About 22 km (13 miles) east of the lagoon are the Seltún Hot Springs **(below)**. One of the geysers exploded in 1999. Walk the boardwalk to explore the steaming vents.

⑨ Selatangar

This village 15 km (9 miles) from the lagoon was abandoned in the 1850s. Ruins are visible through black sand dunes and lava outcrops.

NEED TO KNOW

MAP B5 ▪ The Blue Lagoon, 240 Grindavík ▪ Bus transfers daily from Reykjavík and Keflavík; bus information: www.re.is; ▪ 420 8800 ▪ www.bluelagoon.com

Open Jan–May: 8am–8pm daily (mid-Aug–Sep: to 10pm; Oct–Dec: to 9pm; 24 Dec: to 3pm); Jun: 7am–11pm daily (Jul–mid-Aug: to midnight)

Adm: ISK11,990–ISK79,000 (pre-booking essential)

Icelandic Saltfish Museum: www.grindavik.is
Seltún Hot Springs: www.visitreykjanes.is
Selatangar: www.visitreykjanes.is

▪ The Blue Lagoon's high mineral content can damage your hair – condition before a swim and shampoo thoroughly afterwards.

▪ There is a café at the Blue Lagoon´s entrance where you can buy beverages and snacks.

🔟 ⭐ Geysir Hot Springs Area

The Geysir Hot Springs area lies on the lower slopes of Bjarnarfell, 90 minutes northeast of Reykjavík, and comprises a dozen or more hot water blowholes, including Geysir, the spout that gave its name to other geysers worldwide. The area became active about 1,000 years ago and today the most impressive spout is Strokkur, which you will definitely see in action. Geysir's pool is far larger but count yourself lucky if you see more than bubbles. Visit Haukadalur for an interesting old church and some undemanding hiking.

1 Geysir Hot Spring

Geysir, "the Gusher" **(above)**, has not erupted to its full 70-m (230-ft) height since the mid-20th century, though until it was banned in the 1980s, dumping soap powder into the pool used to trigger a hiccup or two.

2 Blesi

Up the slope behind the Geysir area, Blesi, "the Blazer" **(below)**, is a set of twin pools, one clear and scalding; the other cooler, opaque and powder blue with dissolved minerals.

3 Konungshver

Catch the "King's Spring" on a sunny day and the colours are stunning. The clear, vivid blue water sits in a depression of orange-red rock. Get views from here of the rest of the Geysir area.

4 Strokkur

Strokkur, "the Churn" **(above)**, reliably erupts ten times per hour, its clear blue pool exploding in a 15 to 30 m- (50 to 100 ft-) high spout with little noise. In between eruptions, watch the water sighing and sinking as the pressure builds.

5 Litli Geysir

Often overlooked on the way to Strokkur, Litli Geysir **(below)** is off the path to the left. It was likely once a waterspout that blew itself apart, and is now a violently slushing muddy pool, belching steam and bubbles.

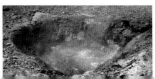

6 Hótel Geysir

Located across the road from the Geysir hot spring, this hotel **(above)** was built in 2019. It has a restaurant (see p113) offering a buffet lunch and an evening menu.

7 Haukadalur Church

This charming red-roofed church lies in a woodland about 2 km (1 mile) behind Geysir. It was built in the 1840s and expanded in the 1930s. The ring on the door is believed to have been given to a local farmer by a giant, Bergþór, whose burial mound lies nearby.

JETS OF WATER

Geysers are formed in deep, vertical, flooded vents known as pipes. The water at the bottom of the pipe comes into contact with hot rock and boils, expanding upwards, while the cooler water at the surface of the geyser forms a kind of lid, trapping the rising water, until so much pressure builds up that the geyser explodes skywards. Watch Strokkur and you can clearly see this lid of cooler water bulging upwards just before each eruption.

8 Haukadalur Forest

Since the 1940s, Iceland's forestry service has planted millions of larches, pine and rowan trees in the Haukadalur valley. An easy walking trail through the area passes through a gully full of waterfalls.

NEED TO KNOW

MAP C5 ■ The Geysir area is right by the roadside on Route 35, about 90 min from Reykjavík ■ Tour buses are available from Reykjavík's BSÍ station. Bus schedule: www.bsi.is

Hótel Geysir: www.geysircenter.com

■ Stay on boardwalks or marked trails and do not step into pools or their outflows, as the water is boiling hot. Falling spray from Strokkur is cool, but you will need a raincoat if you are standing downwind.

■ The Geysir Centre has three restaurants: two of them offer casual meals such as hamburgers, pizzas and soups, while the Geysir Glíma restaurant serves up traditional Icelandic dishes.

9 Geysir Centre

Directly across the road from the hot springs, the Geysir Centre has a souvenir shop **(right)** selling postcards, clothing made from Icelandic wool and unique jewellery, as well as an excellent *supa* (soup restaurant).

10 Bjarnarfell

It takes a steep hike to reach the 727 m (2,385 ft) summit of Bjarnarfell, the hill overlooking Geysir, but the rewards on a good day are spectacular views of the red-brown rock and green fields surrounding the springs.

TOP 10 ⊛ Gullfoss

The powerful two-tier waterfalls at Gullfoss on the Hvítá river present a stunning sight, whether part-frozen in winter, in full flood during the spring melt, or roaring away during the long summer twilight. Their setting in a deep canyon adds to the spectacle, as does the landscape of icy peaks and gravel desert immediately north – quite a contrast to the green, spray-fed vegetation closer to the river. Take care at Gullfoss and always supervise children, as paths are slippery and there are no safety railings or warning signs.

1 Origin of Names
The clouds of rainbow-tinged spray hanging over it gave Gullfoss its name – the Golden Falls. Hvítá (White River) is named after the light-coloured glacial sediment it carries.

2 Geology
The area's volcanic history can be seen on the cliffs **(above)** opposite the viewing platform, with their distinct banded ash layers from separate volcanic eruptions, overlaid with basalt.

3 The Canyon
The canyon continues downstream from Gullfoss for 2 km (1 mile), through basalt columns. You can follow the track along the top or take a white-water rafting trip.

5 View from the Top
The main viewing area, and the safest, is the platform on the top of the canyon **(above)**. Orient yourself and take in the dramatic setting.

4 View from Below
Soaked by the spray, you can really appreciate the sheer scale of the waterfalls **(right)** from this vantage point: the river drops 10 m (33 ft), turns a right angle and then drops again.

7 Plaque for Sigríður Tómasdóttir

A commemorative plaque to Sigríður Tómasdóttir **(left)** recalls her successful campaign to save these waterfalls from being drowned by a dam project.

6 Sigríðarstofa Trail

Starting at Gullfoss, this walking trail uses signs to showcase the hardships of traditional life in the area, which is caught between relatively fertile plains to the west and the sterile wilderness of Iceland's frozen interior directly north.

SAVING GULLFOSS

In 1907, landowner Einar Benediktsson signed away Gullfoss to be submerged by the construction of a hydro-electric dam across the Hvítá river. Sigríður Tómasdóttir, whose father was involved in the deal, was so incensed that she took legal action against the developers. Although she lost the case, public opinion ran so high in her favour that construction never began and Gullfoss was later donated to the nation of Iceland as a special reserve.

8 Visitor Centre

The roomy cafeteria at the Gullfoss Visitor Centre serves delicious, hearty food. The falls are invisible from here but the views show mountains and glaciers.

9 Souvenir Shop

The gift shop at the Visitor Centre sells nothing specific to Gullfoss apart from postcards, but it is still a good place to find T-shirts, designer outdoor gear, books on Iceland and lava jewellery.

NEED TO KNOW

MAP D4 ■ Daily tour buses from Reykjavík's BSÍ station; www.bsi.is

■ Visit in winter when Gullfoss is partly frozen and hidden behind spectacular ice curtains; in summer, the afternoon provides best lighting conditions for photographs.

■ Try the delicious traditional lamb soup at the Visitor Centre café. The warming hot chocolate is also delicious.

10 Kjölur

This 160-km- (100-mile-) long route **(above)**, runs north from here across the Interior, traversing the gravel plains between the Langjökull and Hofsjökull icecaps.

TOP 10 ★ Lake Mývatn Area

Known as Midge Lake in English, Mývatn is a peaceful spread of water east of Akureyri and home to flocks of wildfowl in summer. The surrounding landscape, however, is anything but tranquil, with Mývatn hemmed in by a spectacular mix of extinct cinder cones and twisted lava formations, hot bathing pools, boiling mud pits and screaming volcanic vents. North-shore Reykjahlíð is Mývatn's main settlement, where you can organize tours to local sights and also to the Askja caldera in the barren Interior.

1 Lake Mývatn
Spring-fed and covering 36 sq km (14 sq miles), Lake Mývatn was created during volcanic activity about 4,000 years ago. Lava formations dominate the northern and eastern sides of the lake, while the rest of the shoreline is marshy.

2 Pseudocraters
Looking like bonsai volcanoes, pseudocraters **(below)** were formed by steam blisters popping through hot lava as it flowed over marshland. There are plenty of pseudocraters around Mývatn but the best, covered in walking tracks, are at Skútustaðir.

3 Laxá
Laxá, or the Salmon River, drains out of Lake Mývatn and then runs to the sea near Húsavík. Walk along its banks to see harlequin ducks tumbling in the rough waters between May and July.

4 Dimmuborgir
This weird, tumbled mass of indescribably contorted lava formations makes for an eerie hour-long wander on marked paths. Make sure you visit the drained lava tube known as Kirkja ("the Church") and keep your eyes open for the rare and endangered gyrfalcons.

5 Waterfowl Crossroads
Insect larvae and algae in Mývatn's shallow waters provide abundant food for phalaropes, swans, divers, Slavonian grebes and 13 species of duck, including the rare Barrow's goldeneye **(below)**, which breeds in the lake from May to August.

6 Mývatn Nature Baths

Like the Blue Lagoon *(see pp14–15)*, the Mývatn baths **(above)** offer the chance to steam in the open-air, mineral-rich geothermal waters. The views here – of the lake and volcanic setting – are even better.

KRAFLA FIRES

Earthquakes between 1975 and 1984 opened up a long volcanic fissure at Leirhnjúkur, just west of Krafla volcano, an event that became known as the Krafla Fires. Lava poured out over the plain here, leaving behind a fascinating expanse of still-smoking formations that you can reach and explore on foot from Krafla. It is not an excursion for the faint-hearted, however, as the paths are rough and you need to be careful to avoid some dangerously hot spots.

10 Krafla

Located northeast of Mývatn, Krafla volcano last erupted during the 1720s, when its lava nearly consumed Reykjahlíð's church. Víti **(left)**, Krafla's flooded crater, is bright blue.

7 Hverfjall

This 400-m- (1,312-ft-) high cinder cone is made up of volcanic ash and gravel. There are fantastic views from the well-marked path around the crater's rim.

8 Askja

To the south of Mývatn is Askja *(see p47)*, an 8-km- (5-mile-) wide flooded caldera. The Víti crater nearby exploded in 1875, causing a virtual exodus of the northeast.

9 Námaskarð

Among a landscape of red clay with yellow and white streaks, Námaskarð is an area of violently bubbling, sulphurous mud pits **(below)**. Take great care as you explore.

NEED TO KNOW

MAP F2–F3 ■ There are local buses and tours from Akureyri ■ There is also an airstrip at Reykjahlíð

■ In summer you will need to buy face netting from local stores to protect yourself from irritating – though mostly harmless – swarms of tiny flies. They are worse on windless days.

■ The Gamli Bærinn bistro-bar at Reykjahlíð serves good coffee and food. Other options for cafés around the lake include The Bird Museum, Café Sel and Kaffi Borgir.

Following pages Selfoss waterfall in Vatnajökull National Park

TOP 10 ⭐ Vatnajökull National Park

Vatnajökull National Park, now a UNESCO Heritage site, covers around 14,700 sq km (5,676 sq miles), 14 per cent of Iceland's surface, and comprises the Vatnajökull icecap and connected areas around its fringes. The long canyons and enormous waterfalls at Jökulsárgljúfur, Skaftafell's high moorland and paired glaciers, Snæfell's wilderness and the remains of Lakagígar's catastrophic volcanic event can keep you occupied for days. Hiking, ice-climbing, snowmobiling and kayaking are among the activities possible within this huge park.

1 Vatnajökull
Europe's largest icecap by volume, Vatnajökull dominates the views inland from the south. A dozen or more outlet glaciers slide coastwards off its top **(below)**. At least five active volcanoes smoulder away underneath.

2 Glacial Features
Glaciers are slow-moving rivers of ice advancing just a few centimetres a day (though most of Iceland's are shrinking). Extreme pressure grinds down underlying rock to leave gravel moraine ridges and squeezes out the air, giving them their blue colour.

3 Birdlife
Sandar, or beaches of black sand washed out from beneath Iceland's glaciers, provide nesting grounds for numerous birds, including the great skua **(left)**, an aggressive brown-hued seabird that sometimes preys on weaker birds and their young.

4 Hvannadalshnjúkur
Protruding from Vatnajökull's icecap at 2,110 m (6,923 ft), this peak is Iceland's highest point. You need considerable experience to undertake the 15-hour trek to its summit.

5 Ásbyrgi
This gorge **(above)** is said to be a hoof print left by the Norse god Óðin's eight-legged horse, Sleipnir. Geologists say floods from Vatnajökull carved it.

6 Lakagígar

This 25-km (16-mile) row of craters **(below)** was created by a terrible eruption in 1783. Lava and poisonous gas wiped out farms in the Kirkjubæjarklaustur area, causing a nation-wide famine *(see p116)*.

8 Skaftafell

Previously its own park, Skaftafell was made part of Vatnajökull National Park in 2008. Covering large swathes of accessible highland plateau, the area is home to Svartifoss **(left)**, a waterfall framed by hexagonal basalt columns. Other highlights include close-ups of blue glacier tongues streaked in gravel and superlative hiking along marked trails.

FLASH FLOOD

Jökulhlaups (glacial flash floods) happen when geothermal heating from volcanoes under the ice-caps melts enough water to form a lake. If the lake dam gives way, the water explodes outwards with potentially devastating results. A single pre-historic *jökulhlaup* carved out the Jökulsárgljúfur canyon, while a smaller event in 1996 sent water rushing out from under the Vatnajökull icecap, sweeping away 7 km (5 miles) of the highway near Skaftafell.

7 Fjallsárlón

Although smaller and less dramatic than Jökulsárlón, the Fjallsárlón glacier lagoon is just as photogenic, with its stunning floating icebergs.

9 Jökulsárgljúfur

The name of this part of the Vatnajökull National Park means "Glacier River Canyon", a reference to the 120-m (390-ft) deep and 500-m (1,640-ft) wide slash through which Jökulsá á Fjöllum, Iceland's second-longest river, flows.

10 Dettifoss

Said to be Europe's most powerful waterfall *(see p97)*, Dettifoss **(below)** sits amid a jagged grey basalt landscape. Fed by a river that flows from the vast Vatnajökull icecap, it has a 45-m (148-ft) drop that sends clouds of spray skywards.

NEED TO KNOW

MAP F4 ■ Buses from Reykjavík and Höfn to Skaftafell ■ Tours to Vatnajökull by Jeep and snowmobile from Höfn ■ www.vjp.is

■ Access to Dettifoss is via the paved 862 road (off Road 1); it is open most of the year but can be closed in bad weather. During summer, 4WD access is possible via a gravel road, the 864 (off Road 85). See www.road.is for details. Most sections of the park are inaccessible in winter, and sometimes close due to bad weather.

■ Hvannadalshnjúkur and Lónsöræfi *(see p104)* are open to expert hikers only.

■ There are few places to eat, so stock up on food.

■ Ásbyrgi Visitor Centre is located at the mouth of the canyon and features an exhibition on the area.

🔟 ⭐ Snæfellsjökull National Park

Established in 2001, Snæfellsjökull National Park protects the snowy snout of the Snæfellsnes Peninsula, which juts 70 km (44 miles) into the sea from the western coast. Approximately a three hour drive from Reykjavík with a beautiful conical volcano at its core, Snæfellsjökull is a place steeped in ancient, literary and New Age folklore, though most people who visit today are more interested in the mountain's hiking or climbing potential. Snæfellsjökull also makes a splendid backdrop for delving into the area's fishing history or for bird-watching.

1 Snæfellsjökull
Snæfellsjökull is the 1,445-m- (4,745-ft-) high icecap covering the dormant volcano, which last erupted in AD 250. The white cone of the volcano (below) is clearly visible to the north of Reykjavík on a clear day, rising up above Faxaflói Bay.

2 Coastal Boundary
The rugged coast of the Snæfellsnes Peninsula acts as a barrier between the rougher weather to the north and the generally drier, sunnier south. Strong storms with snowfall on the higher ground may occur throughout the year.

3 Djúpalónssandur
A pretty pebble beach near Dritvík (above), where four heavy stones – "Useless", "Half-Strength", "Puny" and "Full-Strength" – were once used to test the brawn of applicants for fishing boat crews.

4 Hellnar
Hometown (left) of an Icelandic woman, Guðríður Þorbjarnardóttir, who travelled widely in the Middle Ages – as far as Greenland, Rome and America.

5 Dritvík
Some 24 km (15 miles) from Hellissandur, for centuries this bay harboured what was once the busiest fishing fleet in the area. It is a good place to take a break and reflect upon changing times.

9 Ascending Snæfellsjökull

Experienced hikers can spend a day climbing Snæfellsjökull and enjoy the view from the top. It is also possible to sled up and ski down the mountain. However, neither of these activities should be attempted without the assistance of a guide. Get advice from the Visitor Centre or the National Park office before starting the hike.

6 Bird-Watching

Large white-tailed sea eagles **(above)** are occasionally seen in the vicinity of Snæfellsjökull National Park, although these rare birds mainly inhabit the Westfjords. The coastline also supports the usual seabirds and wildfowl.

JOURNEY TO THE CENTRE OF THE EARTH

Snæfellsjökull sprang to fame in Jules Verne's novel *Journey to the Centre of the Earth*, in which a German professor and his nephew decode an ancient manuscript and use the instructions to descend into Snæfellsjökull's crater on a subterranean journey of exploration. Such craters were traditionally feared here as the literal entrances to hell, a belief that left many mountains unscaled till the 19th century.

10 Bárður's Statue

A terrific split stone statue of folk figure Bárður Snæfellsás stands near Arnarstapi. According to legend, Bárður was an early settler in the area and his protective spirit still lives on Snæfell and watches over the village.

7 Hiking the National Park

From Hellissandur, several circular hiking trails explore the lava fields and coastline west of Snæfellsjökull. Expect to encounter little beaches, rugged seascapes, rare plants, birdlife and seals.

8 Arnarstapi

Set at the foot of Snæfellsjökull's southeast corner, Arnarstapi **(below)** is a tiny fishing village, where a rocky arch known as Gatklettur stretches out to sea. The village serves as a convenient base for hikers exploring the national park.

NEED TO KNOW

MAP A4 ■ Buses from Reykjavík to Hellissandur: www.bsi.is, www.straeto.is ■ www.ust.is

Snæfellsjökull National Park's main office: Klettsbúð 7, Hellissandur; 436 6860; www.snaefellsjokull.is; check website for opening times

Visitor Centre: Malarrif; open mid-May–mid-Sep: 10am–5pm daily, mid-Sep–mid-May: 10am–4pm daily

■ To climb Snæfellsjökull you need ice axes, crampons, weatherproof gear and a trained guide. Talk to National Park officers about your route and the weather conditions.

■ Hellissandur's Gilbakki café serves a tasty fish soup.

🔟⭐ Látrabjarg Bird Cliffs

The Látrabjarg bird cliffs are just about as remote a place as you can readily reach in Iceland. Traditionally a farming area, the region has become almost depopulated since the 1960s, leaving Látrabjarg to the millions of seabirds that return here to breed during the summer months. Most people come to the cliffs to see the abundant numbers of charismatic puffins. On the way there is also a worthwhile folk museum and an amazing golden beach at Breiðavík – probably the last thing you would expect to find in this part of the world.

① Látrabjarg Cliffs
The 14-km- (9-mile-) long and 440-m- (1,444-ft-) high cliffs (below) form a colossal bird colony with millions of sea-birds including puffins, cormorants, kittiwakes, razorbills and guillemots, nesting here every year.

② Geology
Iceland's western extremity is home to its oldest geological formations. Each distinct band of the layered cliffs – clearly visible despite the birdlife – records a different volcanic event of the past.

③ Bird Apartments
Species nest at different heights, forming banded apartments: puffins at the top, then razorbills, fulmars and kittiwakes (below), with guillemots on the sheer cliff ledges.

④ Puffins
The most amiable residents of Látrabjarg, puffins (above) nest in burrows at the top of the cliffs. These small seabirds have orange feet and multi-coloured, sail-shaped bills. Though rather tame, they should not be touched or fed to avoid harming them.

⑤ Eggs
Due to their habit of favouring crowded, sheer cliffs as places for nesting, guillemot eggs are conical – a shape that protects the precious cargo contained within them by causing the shells to roll in a circular movement around their tip rather than rolling over the edge.

Guano ⑥

You cannot fail to notice the strong smell of guano, or dried bird droppings, in the air at Látrabjarg. The thick, spongy grass that grows at the top of the cliffs **(right)** exists thanks to centuries of fertile guano deposits. Without them, the puffins would not have anywhere to dig their nests.

THE WRECK OF THE SARGON

In 1947 a British trawler, *Dhoon*, foundered off the Látrabjarg coast in a December storm. Locals scrambled down the frozen cliffs, fired a safety line onto the vessel and winched the seamen to safety. When the following year a film crew arrived to make a documentary about the event, their boat – the British vessel *Sargon* – also ran aground. As before, the crew were saved and the whole event was filmed for real.

⑦ Látrabjarg History

The Látrabjarg cliffs were, until 1926, a favourite summer haunt for local farmers, who would scale the cliffs to collect bird eggs. Puffins were once caught and eaten in large numbers, a practice that continues to this day in the southern islands of Vestmannaeyjar *(see p110)*.

Bjargtangar ⑧

This westernmost point of Europe is marked by the lonely beacon of the Bjargtangar lighthouse **(right)**, a small, whitewashed and distinctly weather-beaten building perched high up on the grassy clifftop. The light-house, which was built in 1948, marks the beginning of the Látrabjarg cliffs. The tower is not open to the public, but the views from the site are stunning.

⑨ Hnjótur Museum

About 24 km (15 miles) from Látrabjarg, this isolated museum gives an insight into the lives of farmers. Do not miss the video of the *Sargon* shipwreck and the aircraft display.

⑩ Breiðavík

Breiðavík, 15 km (9 miles) from Látrabjarg, features a long, golden beach **(below)** – a rarity here as the sand is usually volcanic black. On a sunny day you can almost imagine yourself in the Mediterranean.

NEED TO KNOW

MAP A2 ■ Summer-only buses run three days a week from Patreksfjörður (see website for details) ■ Book in advance: 456 5006; www.wa.is

Visitor Centre: Egils Ólafsson Folk Museum; 456 1511; open Jun–Sep: 10am–6pm daily

Hnjótur Museum: 456 1569; open May–Sep: 10am–6pm daily, by appointment at other times; www.westfjords.is

■ The Látrabjarg road is rough gravel, open only in summer. Check your car rental policy. Unless you have experience of similar driving conditions, it is best to take the bus or a tour.

■ This area is remote. The hotel at Breiðavík is the nearest place for a meal.

TOP10 ⭐ Landmannalaugar Area

Landmannalaugar, meaning "Countryman's Bathing Pool", is a lush hot springs area in southern Iceland, surrounded by a stark wilderness of snow-streaked mountains, ancient lava fields and flat glacial river valleys. Much of the countryside here has been shaped by Hekla, the country's second most active volcano. Excellent camping facilities make it a great spot from which to appreciate the rugged Interior. It is connected by summer-only buses from Reykjavík. You can also hike here along the exceptional Laugavegur trail.

1 Hot Springs
The hot springs emerge into a meadow from underneath a 15th-century lava flow, where they then mingle with a cooler stream. Wade or swim up this stream **(above)** until the water temperature increases, then sit down to enjoy a soak.

2 Mountains
Bláhnúkur, the main peak overlooking the springs, is 945-m- (3,100-ft-) high. There is an hour-long trail to its peak. From there you can view the medieval lava field and ever-changing colours of the grey, pink and orange rhyolite hills **(right)**.

3 Ófærufoss
A beautiful, two-stage water-fall **(left)** bridged by lava flowing through what looks like a small volcanic crater (see p45). Do not get too close to the rim as the soil is soft.

5 Laugavegur
This long and rewarding trail from Landmannalaugar to Þórsmörk spans a distance of 56 km (35 miles), features volcanic plains, green hills, snowbound plateaus and freezing rivers. You can camp or use bunkhouses for shelter along the way.

4 Campsite
The campsite, with grassy spots by the stream and pitches on soft gravel, has showers, toilets and a food preparation area, as well as bins of rocks to weigh down your tent against the infamous gales.

9 Flora
Look for tiny, hardy flowers contrasting with the dark lava walls near the springs. Pink thrifts, moss campion, purple self-heals **(left)**, aromatic thyme, white cottongrass and violet butterworts are common.

6 Ljótipollur
Don't let the name, Icelandic for "ugly puddle", put you off visiting this lake, an attractive blue pool inside a bright red scoria depression.

HIKING LAUGAVEGUR

The Laugavegur hike isn't especially difficult but you do need to be self-sufficient and prepared against possible bad conditions. Warm, weatherproof, clothing and hiking boots are necessary, carry maps and a compass, and bring your own food as there are no shops along the way. Bunkhouses must be booked in advance. Campsites are laid out at about 15 km (9 mile) intervals and campers need strong tents in good condition along with cooking gear.

10 Hrafntinnusker
Hrafntinnusker is a huge "reef" made of obsidian (black volcanic glass) located southwest of Landmannalaugar. Look for weathered outcrops around the lava field and on Bláhnúkur, along with smaller pebbles all over.

7 Hekla
The Hekla volcano **(below)**, towering over southwest Iceland, has been erupting at 10-year intervals *(see p115)*. The road to Landmannalaugar traverses ash dunes and lava fields from the 1970 eruption.

8 Frostastaðavatn
Packed with trout and Arctic char, this lake is a favourite fishing spot. The hike around the shore takes 3 hours and it is a fairly easy walk, except for a stretch over a lava field.

NEED TO KNOW

MAP D5 ■ Mid-Jun–mid-Sep: daily buses from Reykjavík ■ www.landmannalaugar.info

Open mid-Jun–late Aug

■ Book bunkhouses at Landmannalaugar and along the Laugavegur hiking trail in advance with the Icelandic Touring Club at www.fi.is.

■ The hot springs can get very busy at weekends and when the Reykjavík bus arrives between 1 and 3pm. Time your soak carefully to avoid the crowds.

■ In July and early August, you can buy burgers, soft drinks and coffee at the Fjallabúð Café. There are no other places to eat within 50 km (31 miles).

🔟 ⭐ Jökulsárlón

Jökulsárlón is a broad lagoon on the southeastern coast, where the nose of the Breiðamerkurjökull glacier edges down to the sea. The lagoon formed after the glacier began receding during the 1940s and today presents a striking scene, filled by a mass of icebergs freshly broken off the glacier. With a deep, black-sand beach behind you and the white mass of Europe's largest icecap, Vatnajökull, on the horizon, Jökulsárlón is a great spot to stretch your legs on the long drive from Vík to Höfn.

The Lagoon 1

Around 5 km (3 miles) across and fairly narrow, this is the deepest lagoon in Iceland **(right)**. By contrast, its outflow, the Jökulsá, is the country's shortest river.

2 The Beach

Translucent, weirdly shaped boulders of ice **(below)** – the smaller, depleted remains of Jökulsárlón's icebergs – wash downstream to the sea. There they get stranded on the black-sand beach, making for some evocative photographs.

5 Aquatic Life

Jökulsárlón's cool, deep waters attract a variety of fauna including herring and trout, which in turn make it a good place to see seals – often spotted snoozing on ice floes **(below)**.

3 Icebergs

The pale blue icebergs create a natural sculpture exhibition, constantly changing shape as they melt, breaking into smaller floes. Eventually they are small enough to float to the sea.

4 Vatnajökull

The lagoon is a good spot to get a feel for Vatnajökull's vast size *(see pp24–5)*. Breiðamerkurjökull, the glacier that extends off the icecap into the lagoon, is itself 15 km (9 miles) across – but even this is only a fraction of the massive white icefield before you.

6 Breiðárlón

For similar but more remote scenery, head to Breiðárlón, 6 km (4 miles) west along the highway, then 3 km (2 miles) north on a gravel road.

7 Ice Caves
Formed by meltwater flowing into glaciers through cracks and crevasses, ice caves, also known as crystal caves, can be found in Vatnajokull and Langjokull.

8 Birds
Bird lovers should look out for the ground-nesting Arctic terns **(above)** and the bulkier brown Arctic skuas. Both tend to dive-bomb anything that gets too close to their nests.

BRIDGING THE RIVERS

Bridging the numerous deep, ever-shifting glacial rivers that thread their way seawards all along the south coast was such a massive undertaking that the national highway around the country – the Ringroad – got completed only in 1974. Before this, places like Jökulsárlón were well off the beaten track, as the main road between Skaftafell and Reykjavík was, in reality, just a gravel track.

NEED TO KNOW

MAP G5 ■ Visitor Centre: 478 2222
■ www.vatnajokulsthjodgardur.is
■ www.icelagoon.is

Open Apr–Nov; call ahead to book a boat tour as the timings of the tours can vary

■ All buses travelling along the south coast of Iceland stop at Jökulsárlón for around 30 minutes, which is long enough to take in the lagoon and walk down to the sea to look at the spectacular ice boulders.

■ The café at the Visitor Centre opens from 9am to 7pm all year round. It serves inexpensive hot food, snacks and coffee. Delicious waffles and seafood soup are specialities here.

9 Visitor Centre
Jökulsárlón's small Visitor Centre **(above)** has a café selling fast food and hot drinks, and a few shelves of souvenir postcards and T-shirts. Climb the black hillock out front for great views of the lagoon.

10 Boat Tour
For a chance to enter the maze of icebergs right up against the glacier snout, take a boat tour **(below)** from the Visitor Centre. With a bit of luck, you might also get close to the seals.

The Top 10
of Everything

The northern lights above houses
on the outskirts of Reykjavík

Moments in History   36
Churches   38
Museums in Reykjavík   40
Museums Around Iceland   42
Waterfalls   44
Volcanoes   46
Hot Springs and Geysers   48
Places to See Birds
   and Wildlife   50
Outdoor Activities   52
Hiking Trails   54
Children's Activities   58
Nightlife   60
Fine Dining Restaurants   62
Cheaper Eats in Reykjavík   64
Iceland for Free   66
Festivals   68
Offshore Islands   70

🔟 Moments in History

Naddoður discovers Iceland

1 AD 860: Viking Exploration

Around this time a Viking named Naddoður discovered an uninhabited coastline to the northwest of the Faroe Islands. This new land was later visited by the Norseman Flóki Vilgerðarson, who, having spent a harsh winter here, gave it the name "Ísland" (Iceland).

2 AD 870: Reykjavík Settled

Norwegians Ingólfur Arnarson and Hjörleifur Hróðmarsson set sail for Iceland with their families. While Hjörleifur was murdered after he settled at Hjörleifshöfði, Ingólfur went on to become Iceland's first permanent settler, building his homestead at a place he named Reykjavík *(see p76)*.

Statue of Ingólfur Arnarson

3 AD 930: Alþing Established at Þingvellir

All available land in Iceland was settled by AD 930 and regional chieftains found it necessary to form a national government. Rejecting the idea of a king, they opted for a commonwealth. The Parliament (Alþing) was convened annually at Þingvellir, where laws were made and disputes settled.

4 AD 1000: Iceland Becomes Christian

The majority of Iceland's original settlers believed in Norse gods. During the 10th century, however, Norway's king Ólafur Tryggvason threatened Iceland with invasion unless it converted to Christianity. Accordingly, the Alþing of AD 1000 adopted Christianity as Iceland's official religion.

5 1262: The Old Treaty with Norway

During the 13th century, power moved into the hands of wealthy landowners, who plunged the island into civil war. Norway stepped in as peacemaker, and in the year 1262 Iceland accepted Norwegian sovereignty as a semi-independent state under the Old Treaty.

6 1397: Denmark Takes Over

Denmark's ruler, the "Lady King" Margrete, absorbed the Norwegian throne under the Kalmar Union. Later on, Denmark rejected Iceland's claims of autonomy, and in 1661 used military force to impose absolute rule.

7 1550: Iceland Becomes Lutheran

The Danish king appointed Gissur Einarsson as Iceland's first Lutheran bishop in the year 1542. As the nation reluctantly adopted the new faith imposed upon it, Iceland's last Catholic bishop, Jón Arason,

Stained-glass portrait of Jón Arason

took up arms. He was defeated at Skálholt and executed on 7 November 1550.

8 1783: Lakagígar Eruption

A major volcanic eruption along the Laki craters (see p25) flooded southeastern Iceland with lava. Poisonous fallout wiped out agriculture across the land. Famine over the next three years killed one in three Icelanders, and Denmark considered evacuating the entire population to Jutland.

9 1944: Iceland Declares Independence

The mid-19th century saw rising nationalism in Iceland, forcing Denmark to return legislative power to the Alþing in 1874. Nazi Germany's invasion of Denmark during World War II nullified its hold over Iceland, and on 17 June 1944 the country's first president, Sveinn Björnsson, proclaimed Icelandic independence, ending 700 years of foreign rule.

10 2000: Growth in Tourism

Perhaps the defining feature of Iceland since the millennium has been its meteoric rise as a tourist destination. From 2000 onwards, tourists have outnumbered Icelanders, and between 2010 and 2019 there was a sixfold increase in the number of people visiting Iceland.

TOP 10 FIGURES IN HISTORY

1 Flóki Vilgerðarson
The Viking who named Iceland and was known as Hrafna-Flóki, or Raven-Flóki, after his pet birds.

2 Ingólfur Arnarson
Iceland's first official settler, who left his native Norway following a feud with the local earl.

3 Leifur Eiríksson
Son of Eirík the Red, Leifur sailed west from Greenland in the year 1000 and arrived in America.

4 Guðríður Þorbjarnardóttir
After spending a winter in North America, Þorbjarnardóttir made a pilgrimage to Rome, becoming the first Icelandic nun.

5 Snorri Sturluson
The 13th-century historian, politician and author of Egil's Saga (see p84), the Heimskringla and the Prose Edda.

6 Jónas Hallgrímsson
Influential Romantic poet who shaped nationalist pride during the 1800s.

7 Jón Sigurðsson
Leader of the independence movement, he promoted the move for Iceland's political autonomy from Denmark.

8 Hannes Hafsteinn
Iceland's first home minister in 1904, who oversaw a period of modernization and social change.

9 Vigdís Finnbogadóttir
Iceland's first democratically elected female head of state who served as President from 1980 until 1996.

10 Jóhanna Sigurðardóttir
The world's first openly gay political leader, who served as Prime Minister of Iceland from 2009 to 2013.

Former PM, Jóhanna Sigurðardóttir

🔟 Churches

① Dómkirkjan

MAP L2 ■ Austurvöllur Square, Reykjavík ■ 520 9700 ■ Open 10am–2pm Mon–Fri (until noon Sun)

This small, neoclassical Lutheran cathedral was consecrated in 1796, just as Reykjavík, which was previously just a collection of farm buildings and warehouses, began to coalesce into Iceland's first town. The unadorned interior shows off the building's simple proportions to beautiful effect.

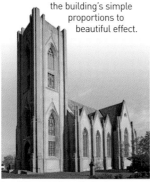

Landakotskirkja cathedral

② Landakotskirkja

MAP K2 ■ Túngata 13, Reykjavík ■ 552 5388 ■ Open 7:30am–7pm daily ■ www.catholica.is

Iceland's Catholic faith was fiercely stomped out in 1550, so it is not surprising that this cathedral dates back to only 1929. Built by famed Icelandic architect Guðjón Samúelsson, it has a flat roof rather than a spire and a functional, plain aesthetic – only the entrance and statues of the Virgin Mary, and other saints, give the denomination away.

③ Bænahús

MAP E5 ■ Núpsstaður, near Kirkjubæjarklaustur

Wedged below tall cliffs, Núpsstaður is a collection of antique turf farm buildings, including Bænahús church, which was once considered Iceland's remotest holding despite its proximity to the coast. Until the 1850s the

Bænahús church, Núpsstaður

nearest harbours were at distant Eyrarbakki and Djúpivogur, and stock had to be transported inland via the highland roads.

④ Grund

MAP E3 ■ Grund, Eyjafjörður

Most unusually for Iceland, this church has an onion-domed cupola topping its wooden tower and Romanesque mini-spires. Although built in 1905 by trader Magnús Sigurðsson, the building has undergone renovations. There has been a church here since the Middle Ages and Grund was once a wealthy holding. The treasures of the church include a 15th-century chalice, kept at the Þjóðminjasafn Íslands National Museum (see p40) in Reykjavík.

Grund church

⑤ Hallgrímskirkja

Vast in scale as it stands proudly over Reykjavík, Hallgrímskirkja is not a cathedral, although it is Iceland's biggest church (see p76). Designed in

Hallgrímskirkja

1945, construction was allegedly undertaken by a family firm of just two people and the building work dragged on, incredibly, until 1986.

6 Hóladómkirkja
MAP D2 ▪ Hólar í Hjaltadal ▪ Regular buses ▪ 895 9850 ▪ Open mid-May–Aug: 10am–6pm daily ▪ www.kirkjan.is/holadomkirkja

Seat of Iceland's second bishopric since the 12th century, this remote cathedral dates back to 1763, though some sculptures – and the ornate altarpieces – are centuries older. The country's first printing press was founded here in 1530 by Bishop Jón Arason, who is buried in a small adjacent chapel within the tower.

7 Skálholtskirkja
MAP C5 ▪ Skálholt, Biskupstungur ▪ 486 8870 ▪ Open 9am–6pm daily; guided tours on request ▪ Adm ▪ www.skalholt.is

Iceland's first bishopric, from 1056 until 1801, Skálholt became an important educational centre and the country's largest settlement at one point. The memorial outside is dedicated to Iceland's last Catholic bishop, Jón Arason, and the 13th-century tomb is that of Bishop Páll Jónsson. Concerts are also held at the cathedral.

8 Þingeyrakirkja

This stone church in northern Iceland stands close to a Viking assembly site and the presumed location of the country's first monastery (see p98). Þingeyrakirkja's medieval alabaster altar was carved in England. The ceiling of the church is painted blue and studded with hundreds of gold stars creating a gorgeous effect.

9 Víðimýri
MAP D3 ▪ Víðimýri, Skagafjörður ▪ 453 6173 ▪ Open Jun–Aug: 9am–6pm daily ▪ Adm ▪ www.glaumbaer.is/is/information

The 19th-century tiny turf chapel at Víðimýri is one of only six surviving in Iceland, with an attractive timber interior. Check out the walls, weather-proofed by stacking thick slices of earth in a herringbone pattern, and the pretty summertime flowers growing on the grassy roof.

10 Strandarkirkja
MAP C5 ▪ Selvogur, near Þorlákshöfn ▪ 483 3771 ▪ Open Jun–Aug: 9am–5pm daily; rest of the year by appointment only

Standing beyond a small seashore hamlet at the eastern end of the Reykjanes peninsula, Strandarkirkja is a picture-perfect 19th-century church, painted pale blue and built on a base of square-cut lava blocks. According to local legend, it was funded by a group of sailors who made it ashore at this very spot during a storm.

🔟 Museums in Reykjavík

① Listasafn Íslands National Gallery

A core collection of works by seminal Icelandic artists such as Ásgrímur Jónsson contrasts with avant-garde installations by the likes of Krístján Guðmundsson and Hrafnkell Sigurðsson. The gallery *(see p75)* also showcases works by big names, including Picasso and Munch. The Vasulka Chamber is dedicated to video and multimedia art.

Exhibit at Þjóðminjasafn Íslands

② Þjóðminjasafn Íslands National Museum

An exploration of Iceland's history and culture, the permanent exhibition – Making of a Nation – shows how the country took shape. Viking graves, medieval church sculptures and 19th-century clothing, as well as modern-day objects are on display here *(see p76)*. There are also regular temporary exhibitions.

③ Reykjavík Art Museum

MAP L2 ▪ Hafnarhús, Tryggvagata 17 ▪ 411 6410 ▪ Open 10am–5pm Fri–Wed, 10am–10pm Thu ▪ Adm (under-18s free); Jun–Aug: free guided tours once a week ▪ www. listasafnreykjavikur.is

The contemporary branch of the Reykjavík

Art Museum's three sites is located by the harbour. In addition to hosting a diverse programme of exhibitions, it also houses a collection of paintings by Icelandic artist Erró, born in 1932. Another branch focuses on the work of Jóhannes Kjarval *(see p76)*, and the third centres on Ásmundur Sveinsson.

④ Landnámssýningin Settlement Exhibition

The centrepiece to this excellent subterranean museum *(see p75)* is the oval foundation wall of a Viking longhouse, with a distinctive underlying layer of volcanic ash, dated AD 871. Holographic dioramas and artifacts, including wooden farm implements and corroded axes, bring it all to life. Look for sacrificial cow bones among the foundations.

⑤ The Einar Jónsson Sculpture Museum

Einar Jónsson's pieces owe a good deal to the nationalist movement of symbolism in art across Europe, with heroic figures in dramatic, iconic arrangements *(see p78)*. One of the favourites is the well-known sculpture of St George resting on his sword, holding his shield aloft, with the dragon coiling behind.

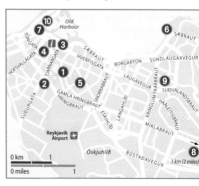

A stone sculpture by Sigurjón Ólafsson

6 Sigurjón Ólafsson Sculpture Museum

Located along the foreshore, this gallery *(see p78)* was founded by the artist's widow. It displays Sigurjón's realistic portraits and modernist, abstract works, ranging from smoothly contoured sculptures to giant installations looking like totem poles made out of driftwood, bronze and steel.

7 The Saga Museum

MAP Q5 ■ Grandagardi 2
■ 511 1517 ■ Open 10am–6pm daily
■ Adm ■ www.sagamuseum.is

This hugely enjoyable museum features characters from the Icelandic sagas, including larger-than-life Vikings such as the violent but gifted Egil Skallagrímsson, Leif Eiríksson, Norse explorer, and the ill-fated poet, politician and saga author Snorri Sturluson. There is realistic detail in the clothing and period buildings, as well as the vivid Viking-age noises and smells.

8 Árbær Open-Air Museum

MAP P6 ■ Kistuhyl 4, Árbær ■ 411 6300 ■ Bus 5 or 16 from Hlemmur & from Lækjartorg ■ Open Jun–Aug: 10am–5pm daily; Sep–May: 1–5pm daily; guided tours in English at 1pm ■ Adm ■ www.reykjavikcity museum.is

A former farm has been converted into an open-air museum of old buildings, farm machinery and period artifacts. The best permanent exhibit is the turf-roofed timber house from the late 19th century. Regular events, when the machinery is fired up and domestic animals wander around, bring the place to life.

9 Ásmundur Sveinsson Sculpture Museum

Part of the Reykjavík Art Museum, this building is an attraction in itself. The real pleasure is walking around the sculpture garden outside, which is full of Ásmundur's depictions of themes from history and folklore, both his early figurative works and his later abstract pieces. Inside are smaller pieces in a variety of media.

10 Reykjavík Maritime Museum

MAP K1 ■ Grandagarður 8, 101 Reykjavík ■ 411 6340 ■ Open 10am–5pm daily ■ Adm ■ www. reykjavikcitymuseum.is

This museum at Reykjavík's old harbour tries to convey a flavour of life on the ocean. Pick of the exhibits is the *Óðinn*, a coastguard vessel docked at the museum's pier.

***Óðinn*, Reykjavík Maritime Museum**

🔟 Museums Around Iceland

1 Borgarnes Settlement Center

The exhibitions (see p83) are in two halves and the entry price includes audio guides (in 15 languages). Upstairs, Iceland's settlement is covered in detail, based on historic manuscripts from its discovery by the Vikings to the establishment of the Alþing in AD 930. Downstairs, *Egil's Saga* (see p84) is brought to life with carvings of key scenes from this violent tale.

Carving of *Egil's Saga*

2 Icelandic Emigration Centre

MAP D2 ■ Hofsós ■ 453 7935 ■ Buses in summer ■ Open Jun–Sep: 11am–6pm daily; Oct–May: by appointment ■ Adm ■ www.hofsos.is

The lonely setting of this museum on the north coast gives some idea of the feelings endured by many 19th-century Icelanders who left for Canada following a catastrophic series of harsh winters and volcanic eruptions.

3 Skógar Museum

MAP D6 ■ Skógar ■ 487 8845 ■ Buses from Reykjavík and Höfn ■ Open Jun–Aug: 9am–6pm daily; Sep–Oct & May: 10am–5pm daily; Nov–Apr: 10am–4pm daily ■ Adm ■ www.skogasafn.is

The museum's collection documents over 1,000 years of history. It hosts a collection of more than 18,000 regional artifacts exhibited in three spaces: a

Exhibits at the Skógar Museum

Folk Museum, Open Air Museum and a Technical Museum. It also houses a souvenir shop and cafeteria.

Herring Era Museum

4 Herring Era Museum

MAP D2 ■ Snorragata 10, Siglufjörður ■ 467 1604 ■ Buses in summer ■ Open Jun–Aug: 10am–6pm; May & Sep: 1–5pm; Oct–Apr: by appointment ■ Adm ■ www.sild.is

Siglufjörður was once – until herring stocks collapsed in the 1960s – Iceland's busiest herring port, its harbour crammed with boats. The award-winning museum documents those hectic times in five different buildings. They offer insights into the captivating herring industry that underpinned Iceland's economy for most of the 20th century.

5 Orka Náttúrinnar Geothermal Energy Exhibition

MAP C5 ■ Hellisheiði Power Plant, 20 mins drive from Reykjavík towards Hveragerði on Route 1 ■ Open 9am–5pm daily ■ Adm ■ www.geothermalexhibition.com

This state-of-the-art exhibition shows how geothermal energy is used in Iceland and its potential as a non-polluting, sustainable energy source. The guided tour is excellent and the interactive multimedia exhibits, which include a display about carbon capture, are fascinating as well.

6 Westfjords Maritime Museum

Ísafjörður was settled in the 1580s and later became a busy port for saltfish. This museum, overlooked by the mountain of Eyrarfjall, is located in the town's 18th-century Turnhús (the towerhouse which acted as a lookout post), documents those times. Photos reveal that the town centre has changed little since the early 20th century.

7 Icelandic Museum of Rock & Roll

MAP B5 ■ Hjallavegur 2, 260 Reykjanesbær ■ 420 1030 ■ Open 11am–6pm daily ■ Adm (under-16s free) ■ www.rokksafn.is

This museum documents the story of Icelandic rock and pop music, covering the likes of Sigur Rós and Björk. Visitors can borrow iPads so they can listen to featured artists' music and try out instruments in the Sound Lab. A new 12-m (39-ft) interactive wall shows a timeline and history of local artists.

8 Langabúð

MAP G4 ■ Djúpivogur ■ 478 8220 ■ Buses run between Höfn and Egilsstaðir in summer ■ Open Jun–Sep: 10am–6pm daily ■ Adm ■ www. langbud.is

The oldest wooden building on Djúpivogur harbour, Langabúð was built as a warehouse in 1790 and is now a cultural centre, folk museum and memorial to the well-known Icelandic artist Ríkarður Jónsson (1888–1977) who taught drawing and sculpture. His works

are on display here. It also has a coffee shop serving brews and snacks.

Húsavík Whale Museum

9 Húsavík Whale Museum

Overlooking Húsavík harbour, where renovated oak fishing boats are now used for whale-watching tours, the Húsavík Whale Museum (see p96) uses videos, relics and skeletons to educate visitors about whales. It is essential viewing before heading seawards to see the whales in the flesh.

10 Viking World

MAP B5 ■ Víkingabraut 1, 260 Reykjanesbær ■ 422 2000 ■ Open 10am–4pm daily ■ Adm ■ www.vikingworld.is

The modern, glass-sided museum just outside Keflavík houses the *Íslendingur*, a full-scale reproduction of a wooden Viking longship unearthed in Norway in the 1880s. *Íslendingur* was built by Captain Gunnar Marel Eggertsson, who sailed in it to New York in 2000 to celebrate the millennium of the Viking 'discovery' of North America.

Waterfalls

Water splashing from under the moss-covered lava bank, Hraunfossar

1 Hraunfossar and Barnafoss

MAP C4

Two adjacent falls *(see p83)*, with very different characters, can be found within easy reach of Borgarnes on the west coast. At Hraunfossar, blue water splashes out from under a lush moss-covered lava bank and gurgles down into the river, while Barnafoss forms a short, savage set of rapids as it cuts through a narrow canyon just upstream.

2 Glymur

MAP C4

Iceland's tallest waterfall, Glymur drops nearly 200 m (658 ft) off the top of a plateau inland from Hvalfjörður, along the west coast. Legend has it that a mythical beast, half-man and half-whale, swam up the waterfall and into Hvalvatn, the lake at the top – where whale bones have indeed been found.

3 Gullfoss

This large, beautiful and always impressive two-tier fall *(see pp18–19)* sits on the Hvítá river around 75 km (47 miles) northeast of Reykjavík. It is one of Iceland's most visited sights, along with nearby Geysir and Þingvellir. In the early 20th century, it was at the heart of the country's first environmental dispute.

4 Seljalandsfoss

MAP D6

Fed by the melting water from Eyjafjallajökull icecap, Seljalandsfoss is narrow and not especially tall, but it drops into a meadow along the south coast with surprising force. Adventurous visitors can take a walk along the path behind the water curtain, for a good soak. Look out for several smaller falls nearby.

5 Dettifoss

Europe's biggest waterfall in terms of volume *(see p25)*, this monster at Jökulsárgljúfur National Park can be heard miles away. The stark setting, where the river drops 45 m (148 ft) between the shattered cliffs of the Jökulsá canyon, adds to the spectacle. Upstream is another waterfall, Selfoss, only 10 m- (33 ft-) high but 70 m (230 ft) across.

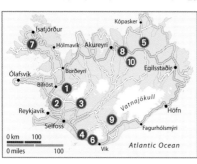

6 Skógafoss
MAP D6

Just walking up along the river to this mighty waterfall is an incredible experience: as you approach, the flat gravel plain vanishes inside soaking clouds of spray and an extraordinary level of noise. Climb a staircase up to the top for more cascades and views out over southern Iceland's coastline.

The cascades of Skógafoss

7 Dynjandi
MAP B2

This waterfall in the Westfjords near Hrafnseyri cascades over several tiers of basalt boulders in a 60-m- (198-ft-) wide, 100-m (329-ft) drop. Crashing over all those boulders gives Dynjandi ("the Thunderer") its name, but views seawards over grassy dales make it a beautiful place to camp out.

8 Goðafoss
MAP E2

Located between Akureyri and Mývatn, this "Waterfall of the Gods" *(see p98)* is where the 10th-century Law-speaker Þorgeir Ljósvetningagoði, who championed the introduction of Christianity to Iceland, disposed of the statues of pagan Norse gods in the year 1000. The ice-blue water channels over several falls, with easy walking tracks between them.

9 Ófærufoss
MAP E5

This waterfall *(see p30)* thunders into the Eldgjá canyon on the Fjallabak Route between Landmannalaugar and Skaftafell. The river flows along the top and drops into the canyon, gouging out a broad, scree-ridden pool before falling again as a smaller curtain onto the plain.

10 Aldeyjarfoss

Off the northern end of the rugged Sprengisandur Route across Iceland's Interior, Aldeyjarfoss *(see p117)* cuts a rough scar across the huge Suðurárhraun lava field, exposing layers of ash and rock that have settled over successive eruptions. Although only 20 m (66 ft) high, the falls are very forceful and electrify an otherwise lifeless terrain.

Aldeyjarfoss, at the north end of the Sprengisandur Route

🔟 Volcanoes

Ash cloud rising from Eyjafjallajökull

1 Eyjafjallajökull
MAP D6

In March 2010, an eruption of the Eyjafjallajökull volcano began at the Fimmvörðuháls hiking trail (see p54). A month later, as it petered out, a much bigger eruption started in the main crater of the volcano. From the 4th until the 20th of April, a vast cloud of volcanic ash spread across large areas of Europe. Many countries closed their airspace, affecting hundreds of thousands of passengers. The volcano remains active, but it is closely monitored by the country's Meteorological Office.

2 Hekla

This large, lively mountain (see p31) has erupted over a dozen times since Iceland was settled, most famously burying a host of nearby Viking farms under ash in 1104. The last major stirrings were in the 1940s, but there have been many smaller incidents since then. In between eruptions, experienced hikers can walk to the top of this mountain.

3 Snæfellsjökull
MAP A4

This stratovolcano (see p104) – one whose cone has built up gradually over successive eruptions – is believed to have last erupted around AD 250 and today it is covered by the Snæfellsjökull icecap (see pp26–7). Unlike Hekla, whose top is usually shrouded by cloud, Snæfell's bright white peak stands like a beacon over the west coast of the country.

4 Öræfajökull
MAP F5

Iceland's tallest volcano is located near Ingólfshöfði. Its terrible explosion in 1362 buried almost a third of the country under gravel and forced the abandonment of farms all along the south coast. Another eruption in 1727 caused less damage, mainly because only a few people had returned to live here.

Lakagígar, southern Iceland

5 Lakagígar

In 1783, the countryside inland from Kirkjubæjarklaustur split open a huge fissure, which belched fire and poisonous fumes for seven months (see p116). It is said that Kirkjubæjarklaustur itself was saved by the actions of pastor Jón Steingrímsson, who bundled the town's population into the church and prayed that they be spared – the lava halted right at the church boundary.

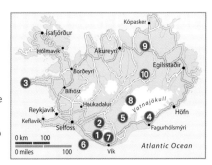

(6) Eldfell
MAP C6

The 1973 eruption of Eldfell on Heimaey, in the Westman Islands, buried a third of the town under lava and the rest under ash. But the harbour was saved – and even improved – by the spraying of seawater onto the lava front as it edged down from the volcano.

(7) Katla
MAP D6

This dangerous volcano lies buried beneath the Mýrdalsjökull icecap near Skógar on the south coast. It erupts on average every 70 years, and the last one, in 1918, sent a titanic flood of meltwater and gravel down nearby valleys. Recent activity in the area, including earthquakes in the caldera, might be signalling the next eruption.

(8) Grímsvötn
MAP E4

One of Iceland's most active volcano, Grímsvötn smoulders away 400 m (1,315 ft) below the massive Vatnajökull icecap. A massive *jökulhlaup* – a volcanically induced flash flood – tore out from under the Skeiðarárjökull glacier in 1995, destroying several bridges. There was another eruption in May 2011.

(9) Krafla

The Krafla Fires of 1975–84 *(see p21)*, a striking repetition of the Mývatn Fires of the 1720s, happened at a bad time: they delayed the completion of the Leirbotn Geothermal Power Station, under construction at the time, for over a decade. However, the new source of natural heat might make it possible to increase the station's projected 60 MW output.

(10) Askja

In 1875, a small vent in the Askja *(see p21)* caldera exploded with such force that it vaporized 2 cubic km (1 cubic mile) of rock, burying farms across northeastern Iceland in a thick layer of pumice and sparking mass emigration to Canada. While Askja itself last erupted in 1961, it is connected to the same volcanic system as Bárðabunga at Holuhraun, which erupted in 2014–15.

Natural Víti crater in Askja caldera

🔟 Hot Springs and Geysers

Geothermal spa water at the Blue Lagoon

1 The Blue Lagoon

Only Icelanders could turn the outflow from a geothermal power station into the country's premier tourist attraction *(see pp14–15)*. The first thing you see when you arrive is people emerging from the milky-blue water with their faces covered in the fine white silt mask that is also sold here as a beauty product.

2 Mývatn Nature Baths

This mineral-rich natural spa *(see pp20–21)* uses its dramatic location on a steaming volcanic ridge overlooking Lake Mývatn to good effect. The water at Mývatn Nature Baths is high in minerals and the steam in the baths is natural, coming up from the earth.

3 Geysir

Now just a flooded crater at the top of a mound, Geysir *(see pp16–17)* once set the benchmark for erupting hot spouts worldwide (even giving them their name) until its subterranean vents became clogged with debris. A big earthquake in 2008 might have cleared some of them: new bubbling and hissing are the first signs of action for decades.

4 Deildartunguhver
MAP C4

Water emerging at 97°C (207°F) at Deildartunguhver, Europe's largest hot spring, fills the skies with steam near the historic hamlet of Reykholt in the west of Iceland. Since 2017 there have been swish and modern bathing facilities at the site, known as Krauma. There are five geothermal baths, two steam rooms and a relaxation area, as well as an excellent on-site restaurant.

5 Landmannalaugar

Popular with Icelanders and tourists alike, Landmannalaugar *(see pp30–31)* is the country's finest natural bathing pool – you just can't beat the feeling of soaking away in the hot stream here as a wall of lava towers overhead and fractured orange mountains frame the distance. No other part of the Interior is so wild, yet so accessible.

Mývatn Nature Baths

Strokkur erupts

and miles of silver-coloured pipes for Reykjavík's water and electricity supplies are visible nearby.

8 Námaskarð

This hillside (see p21) to the east of Lake Mývatn, dotted with roaring steam vents and coloured mud pools, does a fantastic job of demonstrating what a raw and powerful force nature can be. The setting, with a lonely, sulphur-rich orange plain stretching away to the south of the hillside, only adds to the impression.

9 Hveravellir

A famous hot spring on the Kjölur (see p115) route across the Interior, this was once used by Eyvindur, the 17th-century outlaw, for warmth and to cook stolen sheep until local farmers chased him out. A great spot to pause during the rough, 5-hour ride from Gullfoss to Akureyri and enjoy a soak in the cooler spa pool alongside the hot spring.

6 Strokkur

Geysir's stand-in, Strokkur (see p16), is a far more reliable successor, erupting 10 times in an hour – even at its peak, Geysir often lay quiet for days at a time. Strokkur is the largest continually active geyser in Iceland (and the one featured in most photographs), reaching impressive heights on a good day.

7 Hengill
MAP R6

This is a popular hiking area west of Hveragerði (see p112), with hot springs and steam vents. Many of these springs and vents are being diverted for geothermal energy projects – power plants

Seltún, on the Reykjanes peninsula

10 Seltún

Down on the Reykjanes peninsula near Reykjavík, there was a decent geyser at Seltún (see p15) in Krýsuvík, until the entire spring exploded in 1999, leaving behind a grey, bubbling pool. But smaller hot springs still seep out of the hills above, making for an interesting half-hour walk – do not leave the marked paths.

Ísafjörður
Kópasker · Þórshöfn
Hólmavík · Akureyri
Borðeyri · Egilsstaðir
Ólafsvík · Bifröst
Vatnajökull
Reykjavík · Höfn
Selfoss · Fagurhólsmýri
Atlantic Ocean
0 km 100
0 miles 100 · Vík

🔟 Places to See Birds and Wildlife

1 Lake Mývatn

The country's top venue for viewing wildlife, Lake Mývatn *(see pp20–21)* slots easily into a trip to visit Iceland's laid-back northern capital, Akureyri, and a whale-watching expedition from Húsavík. Ducks and other wildfowl are the main draws, but the elusive Arctic fox and gyrfalcon are also regularly encountered.

2 Látrabjarg

Way out in the Westfjords, a trip to Látrabjarg *(see pp28–9)* takes a little bit of planning but you will not forget your first sight of these cliffs, covered by enormous, noisy colonies of nesting seabirds. Stop along the way for a walk or sun-bathe on Breiðavík beach.

Hornbjarg, on isolated Hornstrandir

3 Hornbjarg
MAP B1

At 533 m (1,749 ft), Hornbjarg is the highest clifftop on the isolated, completely uninhabited Hornstrandir peninsula, on the Westfjords' extreme northwest. Like Látrabjarg, it is teeming with fulmars, kittiwakes, razorbills and guillemots. There are regular guided day tours, as well as other scheduled boat trips, from Ísafjörður.

4 Dyrhólaey
MAP D6 ■ Closed 7pm–9am daily

The headland of Dyrhólaey is an easy detour off the highway between Skógar and Vík (there are restrictions on cars but it is open for hiking). Apart from puffins and other sea-birds, come here to view the black, volcanic-sand beaches and the huge sea arch, which is large enough for a ship to sail through.

Skua, Dyrhólaey

5 Jökulsárlón

One of the most spellbinding sights of southeastern Iceland, this deep, iceberg-filled lagoon *(see pp32–3)* between the sea and Breiðamerkurjökull glacier is a great place to spot seals and orca, if you are lucky. The sandy plains on either side are full of nesting terns and skuas – and arctic foxes looking for a meal.

6 Skjálfandi
MAP E2

A summer sailing trip out from Húsavík to Skjálfandi, the broad bay offshore, is certain to put you within viewing range of marine mammals. You are most likely to see seals and dolphins but with any luck you will also encounter spectacular hump-back whales leaping out of the water.

Humpback whale at Skjálfandi

Breiðafjörður
MAP B3

The waters off the west coast are dotted with hundreds of islets and skerries inhabited by thousands of puffins, shags, cormorants and other seabirds. White-tailed sea eagles, one of Iceland's rarest, most majestic species, are also seen here.

Garðskagi
MAP B5

Close to Keflavík International Airport, this little tongue of land overlooks a gravelly beach where you can easily spot redshanks, sanderlings, turnstones, eider duck and other shorebirds – look out to sea for gannets.

The striped red lighthouse was once used to monitor bird migration.

Garðskagi lighthouse

Ingólfshöfði
MAP F5 ■ Hiking tours: mid-May–Aug: Mon–Sat at 10:15am & 1:30pm; tractor from Ingólfshöfði car park ■ www.fromcoasttomountains.com/ingolfshofdi-puffin-tour.is ■ Adm

In AD 874, Ingólfur Arnarson – Iceland's first settler – landed his ship on this cape, located between Skaftafell and Jökulsárlón. Puffins, great skua and other birds nest here in the summer.

Jökulsá á Dal
MAP G3

With river systems and integrated wetlands merging from the highland moors around Snæfell down to the East Fjords coast, this is a summer breeding ground for geese, swans and all manner of wildfowl. Keep an eye open for reindeer herds too.

TOP 10 ICELANDIC BIRDS

A snow-white ptarmigan

1 Ptarmigan
Grouse renowned for its unique, snow-white winter plumage. A popular Christmas dish in Iceland.

2 Puffin
This charismatic bird nests in burrows on grassy sea cliffs around Iceland between May and September.

3 Arctic Tern
A small, graceful seabird that fearlessly dive-bombs anything that gets too close to its nest.

4 Gyrfalcon
A rare, grey-white falcon that once featured on Iceland's coat of arms. Seek it out around Mývatn Lake.

5 Golden Plover
Common grassland bird whose piping call is eagerly awaited by Icelanders as heralding the spring.

6 Raven
Huge black crow with a harsh call and acrobatic flight, considered highly intelligent by many Icelanders.

7 Meadow Pipit
The island's most abundant bird is a sweet songster, though it can be surprisingly hard to see.

8 White-tailed Sea Eagle
Once persecuted by farmers as a pest, around 80 white-tailed sea eagles now breed in the northwest.

9 Eider Duck
Pied sea duck known for its soft, warm down. It is common around the coast and on lakes inland.

10 Harlequin Duck
This sea duck has an unmistakable blue and red plumage. It breeds inland from May until July around fast-flowing streams.

🔟 Outdoor Activities

Hikers on the Laugavegur trail

1 Hiking
Hiking organizations: www.fi.is; www.utivist.is; www. mountainguides.is

Nothing gets you closer to Iceland's raw, natural landscape than hiking across it, following established trails ranging in length from an hour to a week. The pick of these are at Landmannalaugar, along the volcanic trails, and in Skaftafell and Þórsmörk, where you can navigate grassy meadows with wildflowers, lava fields, black-sand deserts and icefields.

2 Swimming
Just about every Icelandic town has an outdoor geothermal swimming pool heated to 28°C (82°F), always with accompanying "hot pot" tubs at 34–38°C (93–100°F), and sometimes with saunas and water slides.

3 River Rafting
www.arcticrafting.is

What Iceland's rivers may lack in size they more than make up for in drama. They tear through narrow volcanic gorges, forming lively rapids. The third longest river in Iceland, the Hvítá is accessible for white-water rafting. The expeditions begin a little distance from Gullfoss waterfall.

4 Fishing
www.anglers.is

Recreational deep-sea angling is in its infancy here and most people fly-fish for trout, salmon or char. A permit is essential: those for trout and char are fairly easy to pick up on the spot, but for salmon you need to apply in advance.

5 Snowmobiling
www.glacierjeeps.is

Snowmobiling or Skidooing is an expensive but exhilarating way to tear across snowfields and glaciers at 40 kmph (25 mph). The best place to try it is at Skálafellsjökull, an outrunner of Vatnajökull.

6 Horse Riding
Riding centres: www.eldhestar. is; www.ishestar.is

Iceland's specific breed of horses arrived with the Vikings. Though somewhat lacking in size and speed, they have a unique gliding gait, called the *tölt*, which is used for moving softly over the rough Icelandic terrain. Many riding schools and farms offer excursions.

7 Jeep Touring
www.glacierjeeps.is

The harsh Interior – a spread of rough lava fields, gigantic icecaps and gravel plains braided by glacial rivers – is navigable only by high-clearance 4WDs (four-wheel drives). Many operators offer tours of this remote landscape in off-road jeeps.

Jeep wading through the river

8 Skiing and Snowboarding

www.skidasvaedi.is

There are established winter skiing and snowboarding venues around Reykjavík, Akureyri, Hlíðarfjall and in the Westfjords, complete with bunkhouses, ski lifts and graded runs. The most accessible are Bláfjöll, outside Reykjavík, and the popular summer slopes in the west of Snæfellsjökull, with winter cross-country opportunities around Mývatn.

Iceland offers many skiing venues

9 Scuba Diving

MAP C5 ■ www.dive.is; www.diveiceland.com

There are several areas to scuba dive in Iceland – the most popular are Silfra and other spots around Þingvallavatn. With crystal-clear, pale blue water and submerged lava formations, Silfra is rated as one of the best freshwater sites in the world.

10 Aurora Borealis Watching

Museum: http://aurora reykjavik.is

The northern lights, or aurora borealis, are solar particles fluorescing as they stream across the upper atmosphere, appearing as luminous curtains of colour. They are best viewed between November and February, on cold nights in years of heavy solar activity, away from sources of light pollution.

TOP 10 PLACES TO BATHE AND SWIM

Bathing in the Blue Lagoon

1 The Blue Lagoon
Surreal blue water, steam and black lava boulders feature at this ultimate bathing hotspot *(see pp14–15)*.

2 Laugardalur
Reykjavík's best public pool *(see p77)*, complete with a separate children's play pool and a steam room.

3 Borgarnes
MAP B4 ■ Open 7am–9pm Mon–Fri, 9am–6pm Sat & Sun ■ Adm
The town's swimming pool has exceptional views from the water.

4 Landmannalaugar
Natural hot springs surrounded by lava walls and orange and grey rhyolite mountains *(see pp30–31)*.

5 Mývatn Nature Baths
Mývatn's answer to the Blue Lagoon, set up on a hillside among live volcanic scenery *(see p21)*.

6 Selárdalslaug
MAP G2 ■ Open 10am–10pm daily
Tiny public pool near Vopnafjörður, beside the fast-flowing green waters of the Selá river.

7 Krossneslaug
Unforgettable hot springs and a bathing pool in the north, near Norðurfjördur *(see p91)*.

8 Hofsós
The waterline of this seaside pool *(see p98)* appears to merge with the ocean.

9 Grettislaug
Remote natural hot tub in the northwest, which was the bathing place of Viking outlaw Grettir *(see p95)*.

10 Laugarvatn
MAP C5 ■ Open 10am–9pm Mon–Fri, 10am–6pm Sat & Sun ■ Adm
Huge outdoor pool at the National School for Sports near Geysir.

🔟 Hiking Trails

View along the coastal trail from Arnarstapi to Hellnar

① Arnarstapi to Hellnar
MAP A4

This short coastal walk between the two small villages offers great seascapes and views of Snæfellsjökull's white cone (see p26). Along the way look out for the statue of Bárður Snæfellsás and nesting Arctic terns.

② Esja
MAP Q5

Esja's 914-m- (2,999-ft-) high plateau rises unmistakably above the bay north of Reykjavík. Its snow-streaked slopes appear to mutate with the changing light – the colours shift from deep brown to pale blue. A return hike from the Mógilsá forestry station takes about 4 hours.

③ Fimmvörðuháls
MAP D6 ■ Summer buses to Skógar and Þórsmörk ■ Trail open mid-Jun–Sep ■ www.fi.is

An overnight trek from Skógar to Þórsmörk (see p26) can be done separately or as an extension

Start of Fimmvörðuháls trail, Skógar

to the Laugavegur trail. From Skógar, climb the steps to the top of the waterfall and follow the river upstream to cross the pass between the Eyjafjallajökull (see p46) and Mýrdalsjökull icecaps, before descending to Þórsmörk.

④ Þingvellir
The mossy valley floor of Þingvellir (see pp12–13) is criss-crossed by easy hiking trails of 1 to 3 hours in duration. Stick to the marked paths, as the vegetated lava flows conceal deep fissures. There are good views along the valley from beside the abandoned farm buildings at Skógarkot.

⑤ Svartifoss
Skaftafell's most beautiful feature, Svartifoss ("Black Falls"), is located on an easy hiking trail atop Skaftafell plateau (see p25). From the car park near Bölti guesthouse follow the signposts for 10 minutes to the falls that drop into a stunning 30-m- (98-ft-) deep gully.

⑥ Ásbyrgi
The top of this huge, curved cliff face (see p24) makes an excellent vantage point from which to admire the north of Jökulsárgljúfur National Park. From the park headquarters, follow the footpaths for 5 km (3 miles) through woodland to the top of Ásbyrgi.

7 Heiðmörk Park
MAP Q6

A 28-sq-km (11-sq-mile) spread of lava, woodlands and picnic sites on the edge of Reykjavík city, with easy walking paths looping through it. Extend an excursion here by making a 3-hour circuit of the adjacent lake, Elliðavatn, to view a variety of Iceland's flora.

8 Reykjadalur

The steamy hills and valleys immediately north of Hveragerði (see p112) make for a good half-day hike from the town, with hot springs along the way (so bring a towel). Keep to the marked path when visiting to avoid boiling mud pots and hidden steam vents, and be prepared for boggy ground and river crossings.

Steaming vent, Reykjadalur

9 Laugavegur

This stunning 4-day hike (see p30) runs from Landmannalaugar, past hot springs and obsidian massifs, to the snowbound Hrafntinnusker plateau, then descends steeply to the green valley around Álftavatn. After passing many glacial rivers, a grey gravel desert at the foot of the Mýrdalsjökull icecap and canyons along Markarfljót, the trail ends in the woodland of Þórsmörk.

10 Þórsmörk

This beautiful highland valley (see p116), with a braided glacial river, is overlooked by Mýrdalsjökull. Carry a map, as few of the many day trails are marked. There are plenty of self-catering cabins and campsites, and daily buses in summer.

TOP 10 ICELANDIC WILD FLOWERS

The vibrant moss campion

1 Moss Campion (Lambagras)
Spongy clumps of this bright pink or purple flower brighten up the muddy, shaley slopes.

2 Mountain Avens (Holtasóley)
Iceland's national flower, whose small fleshy leaves and yellow-centred white petals stand about 7 cm (3 in) high.

3 Arctic River Beauty (Eyrarrós)
Late-flowering plant with distinctive symmetrical, pointed red petals and long leaves.

4 Wild Pansy (Þrenningarfjóla)
Beautiful little plant with violet and yellow petals, which is common locally and abundant in June.

5 Bladder Campion (Holurt)
This white flower is found in small spreads, and has a lilac-pink sac behind the petals.

6 Wild Thyme (Blóðberg)
Tiny, ground-hugging plant with deep red or purple flowers and distinct thyme scent.

7 Wood Cranesbill (Blágresi)
Widespread plant with geranium-like leaves and purple, five-petal flowers; favours woodland edges and reaches 30 cm (12 in) or more.

8 Butterwort (Lyfjagras)
Small, solitary plant with hanging blue flowers and cross-shaped leaves at ground level.

9 Northern Green Orchid (Friggjargras)
Easily missed in the grass, but look for pointed leaves and little white flowers.

10 Purple Saxifrage (Vetrarblóm)
This widespread, but very early-flowering, ground-hugging plant has little pink blooms.

Following pages Interior of Harpa, Reykjavík's Concert Hall and Conference Centre

🔟 Children's Activities

One of many heated outdoor pools

1 Go Swimming

Swimming pools are great places for children to burn off any excess energy, especially after a long car journey. Just about every town in Iceland has a heated pool, which makes it an easy option. Though most of the pools are outdoors, they are especially fun in winter, when snow is falling.

2 Visit the Museums

Iceland's most engaging museums for children are the Árbær Open Air museum (see p41) of traditional farm life; the Saga Centre at Hvolsvöllur (see p112), which is full of swords and dioramas; Borgarnes Settlement Center (see p42), showcasing spooky recreations of *Egil's Saga* (see p84); Húsavík

Children at Árbær Open Air museum

Whale Museum (see p43), with its skeletons and marine mammal displays; and Perlan museum (see p77), with exhibits on forces of nature.

3 See the Birds at Tjörnin

In Reykjavík, head to Tjörnin lake (see p78) in the centre of the city to see whooper swans, greylag geese, eider ducks and mallards. In June and July there are cute ducklings around too, but note that it is forbidden to feed the birds here.

4 Eat a Hot Dog

MAP L2 » **Tryggvagata, 101 Reykjavík**

Eating a *pylsur* (hot dog) from the flagship Bæjarins Beztu in central Reykjavík (there are four further stands around the city) is a rite of passage for young Icelanders, who form long queues outside this unpretentious mobile stand. Why? The hot dogs taste great – though you might want to hold the onions.

5 Visit Reykjavík Harbour

MAP K1

Reykjavík has a busy harbour, with colourful fishing boats and trawlers sailing in and out on a daily basis or hauled up on slipways for repairs. Look in the waters and you might also see jellyfish. Grab a snack along nearby Geirsgata at Sægreifinn (see p65), a charming maritime-themed seafood shack.

6 Go Horse Riding

Short and stocky Icelandic horses are even-tempered, making them child-friendly and a good choice for first-timers. Most of the riding schools cater to children with their flexible schedules and duration of rides (see p52).

7 Picnic at Reykjavík Botanic Gardens

The botanical gardens (see p77) make for a pleasant place for a family outing and picnic, just a short way from downtown Reykjavík. The garden has over 5,000 plant species, divided into several areas including Icelandic flora, foreign perennials, a rose collection and more. There is plenty of soft grass, ducks and geese wandering about, and – in the summertime at least – beds of colourful endemic flowers.

8 Enjoy Whale-Watching

In Iceland there is quite a good chance of seeing minke and humpback whales, orca, sperm whales and even some exciting rarities like blue whales. Húsavík (see p96) is the best place to go whale-watching.

9 Hunt for Trolls

Trolls, the frightening, mischief-making giants, are said in local folklore to inhabit several places in Iceland. They turn to stone if they are caught in the sunlight but their oddly shaped, petrified forms can be seen (if you look hard enough) in many lava fields, mountain outcrops and sea stacks.

A rusted shipwreck in Reykjanes

10 Go Beachcombing

Icelandic beaches are full of interesting flotsam and jetsam, from bird feathers and oddly-shaped pebbles to rusted relics from ship-wrecks, tree trunks (which have floated here from Siberia) and even – if you are really lucky – whale bones.

TOP 10 ICELANDIC FOLKTALES

Statue of Sæmundur the Wise

1 Sæmundur the Wise
Founder of an 11th-century ecclesiastical school, who frequently took on and always defeated the Devil.

2 Viking Treasure at Skógafoss
Legend has it that a Viking named Þrasi Þórólfsson hid his hoarded gold in a cave behind the Skógafoss waterfall (see p45).

3 The Beast of Hvalfjörður
This evil, red-headed whale terrorized Iceland's west coast until it was lured into a trap.

4 Ormurinn, the Lagarfljót Serpent
Iceland's elusive version of the Loch Ness Monster is said to inhabit Lögurinn lake near Egilsstaðir in the east of the country.

5 Bergþór
A friendly giant who lived at Bláfell, near Geysir, and died around 1000.

6 The Lovestruck Shepherd
A favourite tale about a young man who waded across the Hvítá river to propose to a shepherdess.

7 Eyvindur and Halla
Iceland's most famous medieval outlaw, along with his wife, Halla, survived 20 years on the run.

8 The Origin of Öxará Falls
The falls are said to have been created around AD 930 when the Öxará river at Þingvellir was diverted.

9 Were-Seals
Seals are thought to sometimes adopt human form, especially those that swim close to shore.

10 Snorri
The wily thief Snorri escaped pursuit inside a small cave at Þórsmörk – it is near the bus stop.

Nightlife

People enjoying their drinks at Prikið bar

1 Prikið
A 50s-style diner, as well as a bar, Prikið *(see p80)* offers classics such as milkshakes, American pancakes and burgers. During the day it is the perfect spot for people-watching thanks to its location on the city's main shopping thorough-fare, while at night it transforms into a lively and fun hip-hop hang-out with DJs, live music and an energetic dance floor.

2 Kiki
MAP M3 ■ Laugavegur 22 ■ Open 9pm–1am Wed, Thu & Sun (to 4:30am Fri & Sat) ■ www.kiki.is/
Reykjavík's premier (and only dedicated) LGBTQ+ haunt is deco-rated inside and out with a blaze of rainbows, and serves cocktails with names like "You're So Fruity". A welcoming space, it offers DJ nights (usually pop) as well as drag shows, karaoke and live concerts.

3 Lebowski Bar
MAP M2 ■ Laugavegur 20a, 101 Reykjavík ■ 552 2300 ■ Open 11–1am Sun–Thu (to 4:30am Fri & Sat) ■ www.lebowskibar.is
Fans of the movie *The Big Lebowski* will appreciate this quirky bowling-themed bar, with its delicious burgers and 24 variations on the White Russian cocktail. Play "spin the wheel" for free drinks. A movie-themed quiz is held every Thursday (from 9pm) and DJs play every night.

4 Café Rósenberg
MAP M2 ■ Vesturgata 3 ■ 546 1842 ■ Open 11am–10pm daily
One of the city's most popular live music venues, this warmly decorated space hosts jazz, rock, blues and pop, as well as other events such as poetry nights.

5 Gaukurinn
MAP L2 ■ Tryggvagata 22 ■ 958 0212 ■ Open 2pm–1am Sun–Thu (to 3am Fri & Sat) ■ www.gaukurinn.is
This unpretentious LGBTQ+ friendly bar offers a healthy mix of Icelandic and foreign live music with an emphasis on rock and metal, as well as comedy and karaoke nights, drag shows, pub quizzes and poetry slams. There's an in-house vegan diner, too.

White Russian cocktail

6 Bravó
MAP M3 ■ Laugavegur 22, 101 Reykjavík ■ 580 8020 ■ Open 11–1am Sun–Thu (until 4:30am Fri & Sat)
Low-key Bravó, based in the same building as Kiki, is a popular spot for

Reykjavík's younger crowd. It's an intimate bar, and can get crowded as the night goes on and the local DJs rock up. Happy hour can start as early as 11am.

7 **Kaldi**
MAP M3
■ Laugavegur 20b, 101 Reykjavík ■ 581 2200
■ Open noon–1am Sun–Thu (to 3am Fri & Sat)

Convivial café by day and hip craft beer and gin bar by night, this cosy spot is an offshoot of the local Kaldi brewery, which has become well-known for its Czech-style beers. As well as its own brews and gin-based drinks, visitors can enjoy international artisan beers, soft drinks and a limited food menu, while relaxing on comfy sofas.

8 **Paloma**
MAP L2 ■ Naustin 1–3, 101 Reykjavík ■ Open 8pm–1am Sun–Thu (to 4:30am Fri & Sat)

Don't be fooled by Paloma's size, which belies the several venues housed within the same building. The Dubliner is a cosy, "Viking-style" pub, with exposed wooden beams and a bar shaped like a longboat. The upstairs club space plays house and electro, while the basement's bar has a college party vibe where you can play drinking games. The barman will take your requests for songs.

9 **Slippbarinn**
MAP K1 ■ Mýrargata 2, 101 Reykjavík ■ 560 8080 ■ Open 11:30am–midnight Sun–Wed (to 1am Thu–Sat) ■ www.slipp barinn.is

The impressive cocktail menu offered at this bar changes regularly, but the harbour views remain consistently inspiring. Located in the Reykjavík Marina hotel, Slippbarinn hosts Icelandic live music, as well as art shows

and "pop-up" events of all sorts. Brunch is served at weekends and happy hour is from 3 to 6pm every day.

10 **Kaffibarinn**
MAP L3 ■ Bergstaðastræti 1, 101 Reykjavík ■ 551 1588
■ Open 3pm–1am Mon–Fri, 3pm–4:30am Sat & Sun
■ www.kaffibarinn.is

The red corrugated iron exterior, just off Reykjavík's main shopping area, conceals Kaffibarinn's dark interior, with its table-top candles and low-key decor. One of the oldest bars in town, this is a trendy and popular place to meet for the first beer of the evening. There are DJs at weekends and, on occasion, live bands.

Kaffibarinn's distinctive exterior

🔟 Fine Dining Restaurants

Stylish and innovative Holt Restaurant

1 ÓX

Run by award-winning chef Thrain Freyr Vigfusson, this exclusive fine-dining venue *(see p81)* opened in 2018 as an intimate annex of its sister restaurant Sumac. It's been a largely word-of-mouth sensation ever since, thanks to an innovative 16-course degustation menu paired with excellent wines, craft beers and local liquors. With only 11 seats, you'll need to book ahead.

2 Pakkhús

Located in the little harbour town of Höfn, which is famous for its fresh seafood (especially lobster), this excellent restaurant *(see p105)* is housed in an old wooden warehouse down by the water. It provides an atmospheric setting for visitors to enjoy their meal. Don't miss out on their signature dish – the oven-grilled langoustine. They don't have a booking system, so try to get in early.

3 Rub23

With decent steak and good seafood on offer, Rub23 *(see p81)* is also best visited for some of the freshest and scrumptious sushi you'll probably ever eat. Some of their notable dishes are the delicious tempura lobster, surimi crab and Arctic char nori maki. They offer a takeaway service as well.

4 Holt Restaurant

Housed inside Hotel Holt, this warm and intimate restaurant *(see p81)* is filled with unique and original paintings from Icelandic masters. The menu offers modern European cuisine with a seasonal Icelandic twist. The service here is as elegant as the carefully selected international wine list. It is best to book ahead.

5 Fiskmarkaðurinn

Translated as "The Fish Market" Fiskmarkaðurinn is a Nordic restaurant *(see p81)* that has been influenced by Japanese cuisine. Their produce is sourced locally. The sushi on offer is outstanding and the tasting menu, especially curated by the head chef, is great value for money.

A cod dish at Fiskmarkaðurinn

6 Grillmarkaðurinn

The award-winning chefs here *(see p81)* work closely with organic farmers and producers, which is why the dishes here are always fresh, seasonal and delicious. Try their scrumptious salted cod with apple purée and a langoustine salad. They also serve up a good beef tenderloin.

7 VOX

With classy interiors, and a warm and intimate vibe, this well-known gourmet restaurant *(see p81)* heads the trend for fresh local ingredients. The tempting menu here blends classic international dishes with modern Icelandic cuisine. The restaurant also features an extensive wine list.

8 Tjöruhúsið

There's something extremely Viking about this long, low barn of a place on Ísafjörður's waterfront *(see p93)*, with diners crowded together on wooden benches, but there is nothing at all rough about its seafood. The rich, creamy soups will warm you through on a cold day, and the portions of pan-fried fish are generous. For seafood dishes they serve the catch-of-the-day.

9 Sjávargrillið

To savour excellent seafood right in the city centre, try this cosy candlelit restaurant *(see p81)*. They offer a wide variety of set menus that feature traditional Icelandic specialities such as pan-fried salted cod, couscous and skyr. A range of set menus are also available.

10 Fjöruborðið

Famed for its langoustine soups and dishes, this well-known restaurant *(see p113)* is housed in an old timber building in Stokkseyri, which is a 45-minute drive from Reykjavík. Their menu and prices change regularly, and so do the opening hours. It is best to check their website or call for up-to-date information. Book in advance.

TOP 10 ICELANDIC FOODS

Roasted Arctic Char

1 Arctic Char
Freshwater fish with a beautifully subtle flavour. The best come from Þingvallavatn and Mývatn.

2 Lobster/Langoustine
Superb and plentiful, best served as tails with butter and, perhaps, a little garlic seasoning or cream.

3 Salmon
Wild-caught Atlantic salmon is firm and rich. It is usually eaten smoked or marinated with herbs and served as butter-soft gravlax.

4 Caviar
Iceland's supplies come from capelin and lumpfish, not the classic sturgeon, but are just as delicious.

5 Cod
Most often snacked on as dried, chewy *harðfiskur*, but also cooked fresh and used in soups.

6 Hákarl
Greenland shark, fermented in sand for 6 months to break down toxins. Eye-wateringly strong.

7 Brennivín
Icelandic vodka, flavoured with caraway seeds and affectionately known as "Black Death". Use sparingly.

8 Skyr
Similar to set yoghurt, available in any supermarket in a range of flavours.

9 Lamb
This is the mainstay of Icelandic cuisine. Lamb is eaten fresh, smoked, turned into sausages, or preserved in whey after pressing.

10 Ptarmigan
Plump, partridge-like bird which takes the place of turkey in traditional Christmas meals in Iceland.

🔟 Cheaper Eats in Reykjavík

① Bæjarins Beztu Pylsur
MAP L2 ■ Tryggvagata
■ www.bbp.is ■ (Kč)

This Reykjavík institution has been popular with locals since 1937. The stand can be found down near the waterfront and its *pylsur* (hot dogs) are a must for visitors to the city. Your money buys you a traditional hot dog, topped with crispy fried onions, ketchup, mustard and a squirt of remoulade sauce.

② Café Garðurinn
MAP M2 ■ Klapparstígur 37
■ 561 2345 ■ Closed D & Sun
■ www.kaffigardurinn.is ■ (Kč)

This small vegetarian café, which also serves up gluten-free and vegan options, has a set menu that changes weekly. Flavour combinations are inventive and delicious. They offer a range of flans, stews and pastas, but tasty soups (served with bread), tarts and pies are their forte. The "dish of the day" is always excellent value. They serve great coffee and cakes too, so be sure to stop by for an afternoon snack.

③ Jómfrúin
MAP L2 ■ Lækjargata 4
■ 551 0100 ■ www.jomfruin.is ■ (Kč)

Calling this place a Danish sandwich shop does not do it justice: a good

Seating area at Jómfrúin, Reykjavík

smørrebrød (open sandwich) involves a choice of prawns, herring, smoked lamb, cheese and countless other ingredients, served on a thick slice of heavy rye bread, and Jómfrúin delivers in style. Be sure to include the fried plaice in your selection of *smørrebrød* toppings.

④ Saegreifinn (Sea Baron)
MAP K1 ■ Geirsgata 8
■ 553 1500 ■ www.saegreifinn.is ■ (Kč)

A well-known seafood shack by the harbour, this restaurant has a simple yet charming wood-panelled room dotted with nautical paraphernalia. The menu offers excellent seafood dishes such as silky lobster soup. Vegetable skewers and Skyr desserts are also served here.

People enjoying a meal at Saegreifinn

⑤ Lobster Hut
MAP L2 ■ **Corner of Hverfisgata and Lækjargata** ■ **772 1709** ■ **Closed L & during bad weather** ■ Ⓚ Ⓚ

One of few options on Reykjavík's street food scene, this food truck serves local *humarsúpa* (lobster soup) and lobster sandwiches. Icelandic "lobster" is langoustine, a smaller crustacean whose flavour is extremely close to that of its larger cousin, the rock lobster. The hut's generous portions are grilled fresh to order.

⑥ Tommi's Burger Joint
MAP P5 ■ **Geirsgata1** ■ **511 0800** ■ Ⓚ

Opened in 1981, this diner-style joint serves up some of the best burgers in town, with good quality patties and freshly baked buns. The reputation of the Joint has spread since Tómas Andrés Tómasson – or Tommi – first started selling burgers and there are now branches in Berlin, London and Copenhagen. The milkshakes are a must-try here.

⑦ Krúa Thai
MAP M3 ■ **Skólavörðustíg 21a** ■ **561 0833** ■ **Closed Sun L** ■ **www.kruathai.is** ■ Ⓚ

One of the few places left in Iceland where you can get an economical restaurant meal – even if it's only a single course. All the old favourites from Thailand, from panang curry to *tom kha gai*, are served in a relaxed, fast-food ambience. The three-course set menu, which is available at lunchtime on weekdays, is excellent value and the beer is inexpensive. Limited takeaway options can also be delivered.

⑧ Mandi
MAP K2 ■ **Veltusund 3b** ■ **618 8666** ■ **Open 10am–6am daily** ■ **www.mandi.is**

This popular Syrian spot is the go-to place for locals seeking sustenance before or after a night out, as well as those seeking a hearty lunch. The tasty kebabs, falafel bowls and hummus dishes are decently priced too. There are a couple of branches around town.

⑨ Þrír Frakkar
MAP L3 ■ **Baldursgata 14** ■ **552 3939** ■ **Closed Sat & Sun L** ■ **www.3frakkar.is** ■ Ⓚ Ⓚ

Set in a charming building in a quiet residential area, the "Three Overcoats" specializes in seafood, with excellent trout, lobster and soups served with a French–Asian twist. The restaurant also offers dishes such as mixed herring and mussels, as well as traditional Icelandic meals including pan-fried guillemot breast and smoked puffin. Don't miss out on their hashed fish with black bread.

Pan-fried salted cod, Þrír Frakkar

⑩ Noodle Station
MAP N3 ■ **Laugavegur 103** ■ **551 3198** ■ **www.noodlestation.is** ■ Ⓚ

This cheap and cheerful Asian eatery offers three types of noodle soup – beef, chicken or vegetarian – all made from the Thai owner's grandmother's recipe. Grab a seat if you're lucky or order yours to take away.

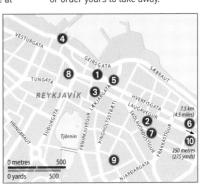

🔟 Iceland for Free

The spectacular phenomenon of aurora borealis

1 Aurora Borealis

Low light pollution in its night skies makes Iceland a superb place to see the northern lights (see p53). Come in winter (they do not appear on short summer nights) during years of increased solar activity. For the best views get away from Reykjavík.

2 Grótta
MAP P5

This nature reserve sits on the tip of the Seltjarnarnes Peninsula, northwest of Reykjavík's city centre. The area has been a reserve since 1974, thanks to its abundance of birdlife such as Arctic terns and tufted ducks. The reserve is also known for its photogenic lighthouse, which dates back to 1947. In good weather, there are views across to the peninsulas of Reykjanes and Snæfellsnes.

3 Berries

Join Icelanders in picking wild crowberries (similar to blueberries) from late summer to early autumn. They grow all over the place, but ask around to find the best spots. Always remember to leave plenty for the birds, who need them to get through the harsh winters.

4 Natural Thermal Pools

Since Viking times, hot springs have been channelled into natural spas. The pick of the bunch is at Landmannalaugar (see pp30–31), but others include Reykjadalur (see p55), found close to Hveragerði (see p112). Here visitors can bathe in geothermal waters, while admiring the views. Pools have strict guidelines on personal hygiene, which all must follow.

Thermal pool at Landmannalaugar

5 Hiking

There are several adventurous hikes within an hour's drive of Reykjavík. The closest is Esja (see p54), which offers remarkable views over the city from its summit. Other trails include a trek up to Glymur (see p44) – one of the highest waterfalls in Iceland – and Reykjadalur, which is a hot spring set in a valley.

6 Wildlife Watching

Iceland is a great place to spy on wildlife. You will find seals and teeming seabird colonies all around the coast (especially at Vík, Látrabjarg and the Westman Islands), reindeer herds in the eastern highlands, shy Arctic foxes everywhere, and rare ducks and other waterfowl at Mývatn lake.

7 Þingvellir Parliament Site

MAP C5

Even if it weren't intimately linked to key events in Icelandic history, Þingvellir (see pp12–13) would still be a spectacular place: a broad rift valley sided in basalt columns where the Eurasian and American continental plates are visibly tearing apart. There's some good hiking here too.

8 Scale Model of Iceland at the Ráðhúsið

MAP K2 ▪ Tjarnargata 11, Reykjavík ▪ 411 1111 ▪ Open 8am–7pm Mon–Fri, noon–6pm Sat & Sun

Plan or relive your travels with this enormous 3D relief map of Iceland, complete with clearly marked glaciers, volcanoes and fjords. Finish with admiring the ducks and swans at Tjörnin lake (see p78).

9 Spectacular Waterfalls

Meltwater from Europe's largest glaciers feeds some mighty waterfalls, where you can lose yourself in the noise and spray. The closest to Reykjavík are Gullfoss (see pp18–19) and Skógafoss (see p45), but it's worth the effort to reach Dynjandi (see p45) in the Westfjords and Dettifoss (see p44), Europe's largest waterfall, in the north.

10 Beaches

Iceland's beaches usually have black sand due to their proximity to volcanoes. The beaches are scenic yet isolated, especially the ones in Wesfjords. Popular white and yellow sand beaches can be found on the Snæfellsnes Peninsula and in and around Reykjavik. Go beachcombing (see p59) for hidden treasures.

TOP 10 BUDGET TIPS

Camping by Seljalandsfoss

1 Carry a weatherproof tent as the weather can change rapidly. Iceland's many campsites are usually well equipped and cost a fraction of a hotel bed. Camping Card (see p127) helps you save money at multiple campsites across the country.

2 A Hostelling International (YHA) card scores discounts at Iceland's many official youth hostels. Visit the website for details (www.hihostels.com).

3 Bring a sleeping bag with you to capitalize on some of the guesthouses' "sleeping bag" offer – accommodation provided at a significantly lower rate than that of a made-up bed.

4 If self-catering, bring your duty-free limit of alcohol and food.

5 Visit off-season (October–April). Some sights are closed or inaccessible, but accommodation and car-rental costs drop significantly.

6 Take advantage of online discounts from Icelandair, PLAY or easyJet. Check websites for more information (www.icelandair.co.uk, www.easyjet.co.uk).

7 Bus passes limit you to specific routes and timetables, but are cheaper than buying individual tickets.

8 Enjoy an inexpensive swim, sauna or hot tub session at public swimming pools around the country.

9 You can cycle around Iceland's ring road in a month, making savings on transport.

10 Buy locally produced smoked salmon, woollen jumpers or outdoor gear – still costly, but excellent value. Don't forget to claim tax refunds for items over ISK 6,000 (see p126).

🔟 Festivals

① Myrkir Músíkdagar
Jan ■ www.darkmusicdays.is

Held at the end of January every year, the "Dark Music Days" festival brightens up Reykjavík's winter gloom with workshops and almost exclusively Icelandic contemporary music performances, ranging from avant-garde to opera.

② Aldrei fór ég Suður
Apr ■ www.aldrei.is

This quirky music festival is held around Easter every year in Ísafjörður. Founded by local musician Mugison and his father, it presents a wide range of Icelandic music, featuring popular acts ranging from the band Múm to local choirs.

③ Reykjavík Arts Festival
May or Jun ■ www.artfest.is

This biennial showcase of concerts, opera, dance and theatre has been held since 1970. For two to three weeks every other year this festival brings together major cultural venues and unconventional spaces throughout the city.

④ Songfest
Late Jun–early Jul ■ www.hafnarborg.is

This annual music festival offers concerts in Hafnarfjordur's Art Museum featuring classical music performed by Iceland's best singers.

⑤ Fiskidagurinn Mikli
Aug ■ www.fiskidagurinn mikli.is

Early August (always the first or second Saturday of the month) sees Dalvík, a nondescript fishing village near Akureyri, draw visitors with its "Great Fish Day", an eccentric social event. Apart from outdoor seafood buffets, look for homes displaying flaming torches – a sign that free fish soup is available.

⑥ Reykjavík Pride
Aug ■ www.reykjavik pride.is

Held annually since 1999, Reykjavík Pride goes from strength to strength, and is now one of the largest festivals in Iceland. For the last few years, up to one third of Iceland's population has attended the Saturday of Pride, when the parade winds through downtown Reykjavík.

⑦ Þjóðhátíð Vestmannaeyjar
Aug ■ www.dalurinn.is

Westman Islands Festival, held since 1874, is for those who are wild at heart. The festival includes camping for four days in a volcano crater, being serenaded by a line-up of Icelandic rock at maximum decibels and skinny-dipping in the sea.

Lively performance at the Aldrei fór ég Suður festival

Menningarnótt
Aug ▪ www.menningarnott.is
One night in August is designated Culture Night, during which downtown Reykjavík is closed to traffic as stages are set up, performers throng the streets and fireworks light up the night sky. The entertainment is mainly professional, with well-known groups participating at times.

Menningarnótt fireworks

 Djasshátíð – Reykjavík Jazz Festival
Sep ▪ www.reykjavikjazz.is
The latest in jazz comes to Reykjavík with a smattering of international stars, but the surprise is the quality and abundance of local talent. Do not miss the Jazz Parade which is held on the opening day.

Reykjavík International Film Festival (RIFF)
Sep ▪ www.riff.is
A selection of the year's best world cinema gets a screening at the well-known Reykjavík International Film Festival. It is one of the biggest cultural events in Iceland and holds events all around town. RIFF includes programmes such as Icelandic Panorama Section and side events like Swim-in Cinema, Film Concert and masterclasses with filmmakers.

TOP 10 ICELANDIC MUSICIANS

Björk in concert

1 Björk
One of Iceland's biggest music stars, Björk is also a unique global phenomenon – and even helped put the country on the map in the 1980s.

2 Sigur Rós
The "post-rock" band Sigur Rós blends elements of pop, classical and folk music, and has unique vocals.

3 KK
Folk guitarist Kristján Kristjánsson is the Arlo Guthrie of Iceland, quite often teaming up with the veteran musician Magnús Eiríksson.

4 Stefán Íslandi
Born in 1907, Stefán Íslandi performed as an opera tenor in the US until his death in 1994.

5 Sigrún Hjálmtýsdóttir
A leading opera soprano and jazz singer, Sigrún Hjálmtýsdóttir has performed with José Carreras and Placido Domingo.

6 Kristinn Sigmundsson
Massive operatic bass, Sigmundsson is one of Iceland's best known international opera singers.

7 Mugison
A slide guitarist from the Westfjords, Mugison, has an astounding voice and performs Iceland's version of fusion-delta blues.

8 Emiliana Torrini
Part Icelandic, part Italian, sweet-voiced singer Torrini was the first Icelander to top the German charts.

9 Daði & Gagnamagnið
Popular group who represented Iceland in the 2021 Eurovision Song Contest.

10 Kristinn Árnason
A brilliant classical guitarist, Kristinn Árnason also effortlessly manages the crossover into rock music.

🔟 Offshore Islands

Imagine Peace Tower, created by Yoko Ono in memory of John Lennon, at Viðey

1 Viðey

Key historical figures have settled on this flat speck of land just off Reykjavík (see p78), among them the country's last Catholic bishop, Jón Arason, and sheriff Skúli Magnússon, who built Iceland's first stone house here in 1755. Today it is a stage for the circular Imagine Peace Tower in memory of John Lennon.

2 Lundey

MAP P5 ■ Cruises from Reykjavík ■ www.elding.is

There are plenty of places called Lundey around Iceland – the name means "Puffin Island" – but this is the closest spot to Reykjavík where you can actually see the birds in question, at least while they are nesting between April and August.

You cannot land here, but cruises circle Lundey daily in summer.

3 Vigur

MAP B2 ■ Guided tours from Ísafjörður mid-Jun–late Aug: Mon, Tue & Thu–Sat ■ www.westtours.is

Out in the Westfjords, this elongated islet makes a great half-day trip from Ísafjörður to see a variety of birds who come to the island during the spring and summer months. Among them are Arctic terns, puffins and eider ducks, whose warm, insulating down is commercially gathered for stuffing duvets and jackets. Only discarded chest feathers are collected and the birds are not harmed.

4 Hrísey

MAP E2 ■ Daily ferry from Árskógssandur (up to 9 times a day) ■ www.hrisey.is/en

A charming island in the Eyjafjörður – one of the longest fjords in Iceland – near the town of Akureyri. Hrísey is well known for its charming village, hiking trails and bird life, including ptarmigans. The waters are also frequently visited by humpback whales.

A puffin on Grímsey

5 Grímsey

Iceland's northernmost point, Grímsey is the only part of the country that is actually crossed by the Arctic Circle. This means that the sun does not set here for a few days on either side of 21 June and does not rise at all in late December (see p95). The island's cliffs are crowded with seabirds during spring and summer with puffins being the most popular, making it a great day-trip destination.

6 Drangey
MAP D2

Part of a dead volcano, this 180-m- (590-ft-) high, sheer-sided palagonite rock has become a nesting colony for thousands of seabirds, including puffins, guillemots, gannets, kittiwakes and fulmars. A path leads to the top of the island and offers stellar views across the fjörd. Boat tours operate here regularly in summer and on request in winter.

7 Flatey
MAP E2 ■ Daily ferry from Stykkishólmur–Brjánslækur ■ www.seatours.is

Although hard to believe, this sleepy island, half-way across Breiðafjörður between Snæfellsnes and the Westfjords, housed an important 12th-century monastery. Later it became known for the *Flateyjarbók*, an illuminated medieval manuscript featuring the *Greenland Saga*, which was discovered on the island but is now

kept in Reykjavík's Culture House. The east of the island is a reserve for nesting seabirds.

8 Westman Islands

Known in Icelandic as Vestmannaeyjar, this archipelago (see p110) comprises 15 islands and 30 rock stacks found off the country's south coast. The islands are well-known for their natural beauty and large puffin population, as well as for Surtsey. This small island – now a special UNESCO reserve – was formed here following an underwater volcanic eruption in 1963.

9 Eldey
MAP B5

About 15 km (9 miles) off Iceland's southwesternmost tip, Eldey's distinctive, rocky, sheer-sided cliffs rise 77 m (250 ft) straight out of the Atlantic. The top forms a level plat-form, home to Europe's largest gannet colony. Sadly, this is also where the last known pair of great auks were killed in 1844.

10 Heimaey
MAP C6 ■ Daily ferry to Herjólfur from Þorlákshöfn or Landeyjahöfn ■ www.herjolfur.is

This 3-km- (2-mile-) long island off the south coast has enough birds, volcanoes, Viking history and walks to occupy you for a couple of sunny days. The town of the same name occupies the north end of the island and is famous for being nearly annihilated during a volcanic eruption in 1973.

Heimaey, a picturesque island town

Iceland
Area by Area

**Multicoloured volcanic landscape,
Landmannalaugar, South Iceland**

Reykjavík	**74**
West Iceland and the Snæfellsnes Peninsula	**82**
The Westfjords	**88**
North Iceland	**94**
East Iceland	**100**
South Iceland	**108**
The Highland Interior	**114**

🔟 Reykjavík

**Statue,
National
Museum**

The Reykjavík area covers the city centre, plus a handful of satellite suburbs. The city's tiny core consists of a historic precinct of lanes near the old harbour, easily covered on foot in a day. While the municipal buildings are made of stone or concrete – practical protection against the fierce winter winds – most of the area is residential, comprising wooden houses, weatherproofed in brightly coloured corrugated iron. Here you will find most of Iceland's shops, cafés, restaurants and nightclubs, alongside museums and galleries. A distinctive landmark is Öskjuhlíð hill, with panoramic views of more distant sights and suburbs.

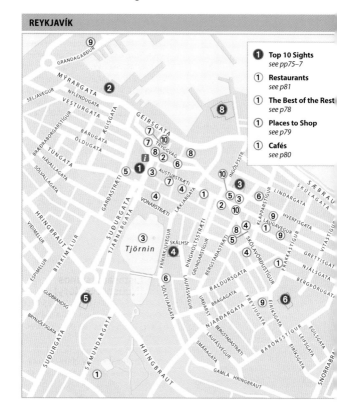

REYKJAVÍK

1 **Top 10 Sights**
see pp75–7

1 **Restaurants**
see p81

1 **The Best of the Rest**
see p78

1 **Places to Shop**
see p79

1 **Cafés**
see p80

1 Landnámssýningin (Settlement Exhibition)

MAP K2 ■ Aðalstræti 16 ■ 411 6370
■ Open 10am–5pm daily ■ Adm
■ www.reykjavikcitymuseum.is

This impressive exhibition comprises the in-situ remains of a large Viking-age longhouse, possibly belonging to Iceland's first settler, Norwegian Ingólfur Arnarson (see p36), who sailed to Iceland around AD 870. There are virtually no other contemporary remains in such good condition. Its location under the capital's streets makes it even more incredible.

2 Historic Midtown and Harbour

MAP K1

Midtown is the site of Iceland's first Viking settlement and the city's

Historic buildings, midtown Reykjavík

oldest building (on Lækjatorg Square). A statue of Jón Sigurðsson (see p37) faces the 1881 Parliament House, which replaced the Alþing's home at Þingvellir. The Old Harbour is home to a slew of fishing boats and the fascinating Saga Museum (see p41).

3 Safnahúsið (Culture House)

MAP L2 ■ Hverfisgata 15 ■ 530 2210
■ Open May–mid-Sep: 10am–5pm daily; mid-Sep–Apr: 10am–5pm Tue–Sun ■ Adm ■ Guided tours available
■ www.nationalmuseum.is

As a part of the National Museum of Iceland, Safnahúsið gives an insight into the country's heritage through paintings, objects and archival materials, such as books and maps.

Medieval manuscript, Safnahúsið

4 Listasafn Íslands (National Gallery)

MAP L3 ■ Fríkirkjuvegur 7 ■ 515 9600
■ Open summer: 10am–5pm daily; winter: 10am–5pm Tue–Sun ■ www. listasafn.is

The nation's main collection of art concentrates on early 20th-century Icelandic painters. Listasafn Íslands (see p40) continually rotates the estimated 10,000 works.

5 Þjóðminjasafn Íslands (National Museum)

MAP K3 ▪ Suðurgata 41 ▪ 530 2200 ▪ Open May–mid-Sep: 10am–5pm daily; mid-Sep–Apr: 10am–5pm Tue–Sun ▪ Adm ▪ www.national museum.is

Documenting Iceland's history and culture from the earliest evidence of settlement to the present, the museum (see p40) offers interactive learning opportunities for visitors. Whether it is Viking graves, medieval statues from churches or modern-day objects, there is something for everyone in this interesting exhibition covering the museum's two floors.

6 Hallgrímskirkja

MAP M3 ▪ Hallgrímstorg 1 ▪ 510 1000 ▪ Open 10am–5pm daily ▪ Church: free; tower: adm ▪ www.hallgrimskirkja.is

The largest in Iceland, this 74-m- (240-ft-) high church took 40 years to build and resembles a volcanic formation, covered in hexagonal pillars. The sound of the stunning church organ, fitted with 5,275 pipes, is a highlight. Take the lift to the tower for views over Reykjavík's colourful rooftops and Leifur Eiríksson's statue.

Leifur Eiríksson

THE SETTLEMENT OF REYKJAVÍK

When Ingólfur Arnarson first saw Iceland on his voyage from Norway in AD 870, he threw overboard his valuable wooden seat-posts and vowed to settle wherever they washed up. They were finally found in a broad, fertile, steamy inlet on the island's southwest, which Ingólfur named Reykjavík ("Smoky Bay").

7 Kjarvalsstaðir (Reykjavík Art Museum)

MAP N4 ▪ Flókagata 24 ▪ 411 6420 ▪ Open 10am–5pm daily ▪ Guided tours by arrangement ▪ Adm ▪ www.listasafnreykjavikur.is

Jóhannes Kjarval (1885–1972), born in a tiny village in the north-east, studied painting in Europe. On returning to Iceland he began incorporating the landscapes into his brightly coloured paintings. Though considered Iceland's greatest artist, his work often controversially blended folklore, Christianity and paganism. Apart from his works, this museum also exhibits contemporary Icelandic and foreign art.

8 Harpa

MAP L2 ▪ Austurbakki 2 ▪ 528 5050 ▪ Guided tours year-round ▪ www.harpa.is

Harpa – Reykjavík's Concert Hall and Conference Centre – is the most important performance venue in the

Harpa, Reykjavík's Concert Hall and Conference Centre

country, and is home to the Iceland Symphony Orchestra, the Icelandic Opera and the Reykjavík Big Band. With a façade by artist Olafur Eliasson, it is a symbol of the revitalization of Reykjavík's historic waterfront and of Iceland's dynamism.

Perlan's mirrored-glass dome

9 Perlan
MAP M6 ▪ Öskjuhlið ▪ Bus 18 from Hlemmur ▪ Exhibition: 8am–7pm daily; observation deck: 8am–8pm daily ▪ Adm ▪ www.perlan.is

Just south of the city centre, wooded Öskjuhlíð hill is covered in a network of walking and cycling tracks. The summit is capped by the mirrored-glass dome of Perlan ("the Pearl"). This imaginative building, made from converted cylindrical water tanks, has fabulous city panoramas from the outside observation deck. Inside, a permanent exhibition called Wonders of Iceland provides insights into the country's nature through interactive technology and design.

10 Laugardalur Park and Recreation Area
MAP R4 ▪ Laugardalur ▪ Bus 14 from Hlemmur ▪ Pool: 411 5100 ▪ Open Apr–Aug: 6:30am–10pm Mon–Fri, 8am–10pm Sat & Sun ▪ Park free; activities adm

East of the city centre, Laugardalur Park is a great spot to join local families relaxing. The Botanic Gardens have a wealth of local and international plants, and a pleasant rock garden. You can skate in winter at the adjacent sports centre. The naturally heated 50-m- (164-ft-) long outdoor pool, with three smaller play pools and hot tubs, is open year-round.

▶ MORNING

Kick off the day the way many Icelanders do – by having a swim at the central Sundhöllin indoor pool. After a coffee at **Kaffitár** on Bankastræti, head for the Þjóðminjasafn Íslands and get a solid grounding in Icelandic history, though don't burn out by trying to cover it all on a single trip. Amble down to get some fresh air and admire the birds at Tjörnin *(see p78)*, before ducking inside City Hall for a look at the giant relief map of the country, or to catch a lunchtime concert. Sit out on the grass at Austurvöllur Square to admire the humble Reykjavík Cathedral, the Art Deco Hótel Borg and the Parliament House. Then spend half an hour among Viking remains at the excellent **Landnámssýningin** *(see p75)*, which is located nearby.

AFTERNOON

Reboot your energy levels with a plate of duck Wellington at the **Duck & Rose** *(see p80)*, then shop for jewellery, clothes or souvenirs along **Laugavegur** *(see p30)*. Head uphill, past a street of colourful houses on Klapparstígur, to take in the cityscape from the top of **Hallgrímskirkja**. If you have room for another museum, soak up some Saga-Age ambience at **Safnahúsið** *(see p75)*. Walk north to **Harpa** to take in a concert, or to see the striking Solar Voyager sculpture and historic **Höfði House** *(see p78)*. After dinner, visit some of the city's bars – **Prikið** *(see p80)*, in the city centre, is the best place to start.

The Best of the Rest

1 Norræna Húsið
MAP K4 ■ Sæmundargata 11 ■ 551 7030 ■ Library open: 10am–5pm Tue–Sun; exhibition room: times vary, check website for details ■ www.nordichouse.is

Exhibitions, concerts and a library devoted to Nordic culture.

Höfði, the Nordic House

2 Höfði House
MAP P2 ■ Borgartún

Mikhail Gorbachev and Ronald Reagan ended the Cold War in this house in 1986. Nearby sculpture *Solar Voyager* honours Viking travels.

3 Tjörnin
MAP K3

Locals bring their children to spot the ducks, geese and swans at this lake in the city centre.

4 Alþingishúsið
MAP L2

Viðey seabird

■ Austurvöllur ■ 563 0500 ■ Times vary, check website ■ www.althingi.is

This building houses the national parliament. Founded at Þingvellir in AD 930, it relocated here in 1881.

5 Sigurjón Ólafsson Sculpture Museum
MAP Q1 ■ Laugarnestangi 70 ■ Buses 12 & 15 ■ 553 2906 ■ Open Jun–Sep: 1–5pm daily (Oct–May: to 5pm Sat & Sun) ■ Closed Dec & Jan ■ www.lso.is

Once the studio of Sigurjón Ólafsson, this building displays his sculptures and hosts summer concerts.

6 Ásmundur Sveinsson Sculpture Museum
MAP Q4 ■ Sigtún ■ 411 6430 ■ Open May–Sep: 10am–5pm daily; Oct–Apr: 1–5pm daily ■ Adm ■ www.artmuseum.is

With its Mediterranean and African influences, this building is as interesting as the works of the renowned sculptor displayed here.

7 Hafnarfjörður
MAP P6 ■ Bus 1 from Hamraborg ■ www.hafnarfjordur.is, www.fjorukrain.is

This seaside suburb of Reykjavík is home to good eateries, including a Viking-themed restaurant and hotel.

8 Viðey
MAP P5 ■ Mid-May–Sep: 8 ferries daily from Skarfabakka, and 2 daily from Reykjavík's Old Harbour and Harpa ■ www.videy.com

Just off Reykjavík, this grassy isle (*see p70*) boasts Iceland's oldest stone building (now a restaurant), thousands of seabirds and the Imagine Peace Tower.

9 The Einar Jónsson Sculpture Museum
MAP M3 ■ Eiríksgata ■ Open 10am–5pm Tue–Sun ■ Adm ■ www.lej.is

Plaster and bronze statues by Iceland's first modern sculptor, Einar Jónsson (1874–1954), are on display here.

10 Nauthólsvík Geothermal Beach
MAP M6 ■ Changing rooms: open mid-May–mid Aug: 11am–7pm Mon–Thu (to 4pm Sat) ■ www.nautholsvik.is/en

This yellow-sand beach, set on the waterfront south of the city centre, comes complete with open-air hot tubs and pool. The beach's geothermal pumps try to keep the water in the hot tubs and pool at around 18°C.

Places to Shop

① **Aurum**
MAP L2 ■ Banakstræti 4
■ 551 2770 ■ www.aurum.is
Guðbjörg Kristín Ingvarsdóttir's jewellery is modelled on the landscape of Iceland, using precious metals to create delicate, fluid designs that are both modern and timeless.

② **The Viking**
MAP L2 ■ Hafnarstræsti 1–3
■ 551 1250
Known for its friendly service and long opening hours, this gift shop has been in the same family for over 50 years. Now a chain with five stores across Iceland.

③ **Thorvaldsens Bazar**
MAP L2 ■ Austurstræti 4
■ 551 3509 ■ www.thorvaldsens.is
This charity shop has been in business for over a century and specializes in handmade Icelandic goods – knitted jumpers, local woodcarvings and silver jewellery.

④ **Penninn Eymundsson**
MAP L3 ■ Skólavörðustíg 11
■ 540 2350
This excellent bookshop offers a range of maps, from road atlases to hiking maps, as well as English-language books on Iceland and stationery. There is also a good café.

⑤ **12 Tónar**
MAP L3 ■ Skólavörðustíg 15
■ 511 5656
Selling music CDs and vinyl, this shop also hosts concerts (especially during the summer) by an eclectic inventory of local artists covering jazz, classical and pop.

⑥ **AKKÚRAT**
MAP L2 ■ Hverfisgata 34
■ 895 4452 ■ akkurat.is
The products at this boutique store range from clothes to homeware and have been created by contemporary Icelandic and Nordic designers.

Paper bowls at Kirsuberjatréð

⑦ **Kirsuberjatréð**
MAP L2 ■ Vesturgata 4
■ 562 8990 ■ www.kirs.is
This unique store, run by a women's cooperative, offers distinctly Icelandic garments, fish-skin accessories, glassware, jewellery and gifts.

⑧ **Michelsen 1909**
MAP L2 ■ Tryggvagata 25
■ 511 1900 ■ www.michelsen.is
Great old-style watchmaker, with a workshop full of pre-digital timepieces in the process of being repaired. Sells contemporary brands such as Rolex, TAG Heuer and more.

⑨ **Vínberið**
MAP K1 ■ Laugavegur 43
■ 551 2475 ■ vinberid.is
This family-run confectionary store was founded in 1976 and caters to people with a sweet tooth. They feature a wide range of handmade chocolates and local sweets.

⑩ **Kolaportið Flea Market**
MAP L2 ■ Tryggvagata 19 ■ 562 5030
■ Open 11am–5pm Sat & Sun
Join the locals in spending a couple of hours sifting through acres of household junk at this market and you might uncover unexpectedly stylish designer clothing or eclectic antiques. Good home-grown vegetables are for sale here, too.

See map on pp74–5

Cafés

① Reykjavík Roasters
MAP M3 ▪ Kárastígur 1
▪ 517 5535 ▪ Open 8:30am–5pm
Mon–Fri (from 9am Sat, 10am Sun)
▪ www.reykjavikroasters.is
Set in an old building, this café serves immaculate coffees made with beans roasted in-house.

② Prikið
MAP L2 ▪ Bankastræti 12 ▪ 551 2866 ▪ Open 8am–1am Mon–Thu, 11am–4:30am Fri & Sat, noon–1am Sun ▪ www.prikid.is
This café-diner (see p60), popular with an arty crowd, becomes a bar at night. There are hip-hop DJs on weekends.

③ Kaffihus Vesturbaejar
MAP J3 ▪ Melhagi 20, 107 Reykjavík ▪ 551 0623 ▪ Open 8am–11pm Mon–Fri (from 9am Sat–Sun) ▪ www.kaffihusvesturbaejar.is/
Try the coffees and baked pastries at this bistro. There is also a dinner menu and bar area for the evenings.

④ Café Babalú
MAP L3 ▪ 22, Skólavörðustígur
▪ 555 8845
A quirky and colourful space, this café serves great coffee and cakes. It is frequented by a hip local crowd.

⑤ Grái Kötturinn
MAP L2 ▪ Hverfisgata 16a
▪ 551 1544 ▪ Open 7:30am–2:30pm
Mon–Fri, 8am–2:30pm Sat & Sun
Huge breakfasts are served at this trendy basement café.

⑥ Hornið
MAP L2 ▪ Hafnarstræti 15
▪ 551 3340
In business since 1979, this family-run, cosy Italian pizzeria was one of the first places to serve espresso in Iceland. Their fresh seafood pastas are superb.

⑦ Duck & Rose
MAP L2 ▪ Austurstræti 14
▪ 551 1020 ▪ Open 11:30am–10pm daily ▪ www.duckandrose.is/
This café and restaurant serves a classic European menu (think duck Wellington or duck wings with chicken liver créme brulée) made with Icelandic ingredients. The weekend brunch (11:30am–3pm) is popular, not least for its bottomless mimosas.

⑧ Fjallkonan
MAP L2 ▪ Hafnarstræti 1–3
▪ 555 0950 ▪ Open 11:30am–11pm daily ▪ www.fjallkona.is
Casual space that serves as café, bar and restaurant. There are hearty lunch and brunch options including soups, burgers, salads and classic fish dishes.

⑨ Sandholt
MAP M3 ▪ Laugavegur 36
▪ 551 3524
Tasty sourdough breads, quiches, handmade chocolates, sandwiches and superb coffee are all served at this family-run bakery.

⑩ Mokka
MAP L3
▪ Skólavörðustíg 3a
▪ 552 1174
The capital's oldest café (it opened in 1958), the no-frills Mokka is credited with spearheading caffeine culture in Iceland, and is known for it's waffles. It regularly hosts art exhibitions too.

Grái Kötturinn

Restaurants

PRICE CATEGORIES
For a three-course meal for one with half
a bottle of wine (or equivalent meal),
including taxes and extra charges.

Ⓚ under ISK5,000   ⓀⓀ ISK5,000–9,000
ⓀⓀⓀ over ISK9,000

① ÓX
MAP M3 ▪ Laugavegur 28
▪ 537 9900 ▪ Open from 7pm Thu–Sat
▪ www.ox.restaurant

An intimate restaurant *(see p62)* on
the high street, offering an exclusive
dining experience. Book ahead.

② VOX
MAP R4 ▪ Hilton Reykjavík
Nordica, Suðurlandsbraut 2, 108
Reykjavík ▪ 444 5050 ▪ www.vox.is
▪ ⓀⓀⓀ

This elegant fine dining restaurant
(see p62) offers dishes inspired by both
Icelandic and international cuisine,
as well as excellent wine pairings.

③ Punk
MAP L2 ▪ Hverfisgata 20 ▪ 537
7865 ▪ www.punkrestaurant.is ▪ ⓀⓀ

A colourful, swanky restaurant, Punk
offers interesting fusion dishes that
blend international and Icelandic
cuisine. There is also a fine selection
of cocktails and wines.

④ Grillmarkaðurinn
MAP L2 ▪ Lækjargata 2A, 101
Reykjavík ▪ 571 7777 ▪ Closed Sat
& Sun L ▪ www.grillmarkadurinn.is
▪ ⓀⓀⓀ

The menu here *(see p62)* introduces
dishes that are a smooth blend of
the traditional and the modern.

⑤ Fiskmarkaðurinn
MAP K2 ▪ Aðalstræti 12, 101
Reykjavík ▪ 578 8877 ▪ Open 5:30–
10:30pm daily ▪ ⓀⓀⓀ

Enjoy Japanese cuisine at this
restaurant *(see p63)*. The menu
features a range of seafood dishes
including sushi, maki and nigiri.
Vegetarian options are available.

⑥ Holt Restaurant
MAP L3 ▪ Hótel Holt,
Bergstaðastræti 37, 101 Reykjavík
▪ 552 5700 ▪ Closed Sun–Tue ▪ ⓀⓀ

Hearty dishes are served in an upscale
dining room *(see p62)*, which features a
collection of Icelandic art. Book ahead.

⑦ Fiskfelagið
MAP K2 ▪ Vesturgata 2a
▪ Open 11:30am–10:30pm Mon–Thu
(to 11:30pm Fri), 5–11:30pm Sat &
Sun ▪ www.fiskfelagid.is ▪ ⓀⓀⓀ

The exquisite menu here ranges from
Arctic char to pan-fried lamb ribeye.

Cosy interior of Sjávargrillið

⑧ Sjávargrillið
MAP L3 ▪ Skólavörðustíg 14,
101 Reykjavík ▪ 571 1100 ▪ Closed
Mon–Sat D, Sun L ▪ www.sjavar
grillid.is ▪ ⓀⓀ

Visit this classy candlelit restaurant
(see p63) to experience fine dining.

⑨ Sumac Grill + Drinks
MAP M3 ▪ Laugavegur 28
▪ Open 5:30–10pm Tue–Thu, 5–11pm
Fri & Sat ▪ www.sumac.is ▪ ⓀⓀ

On offer at Sumac is a delicious
fusion of Moroccan and Lebanese
cuisine with an Icelandic edge.

⑩ Dill
MAP L2 ▪ Hverfisgata 12
▪ 552 1522 ▪ ⓀⓀⓀ

Dill specializes in New Nordic
Cuisine, pairing traditional dishes
such as arctic char, lamb shanks
and pork belly with barley,
berries and kale.

See map on pp74–5 ←

🔟 West Iceland and the Snæfellsnes Peninsula

Heading north from Reykjavík, the highway follows the western coastline, famous for its stormy weather. Beyond Hvalfjörður and the exceptional Glymur falls are Akranes and Borgarnes, once home to the notorious Viking Egill Skallagrímsson. The 13th-century historian Snorri Sturluson lived (and was murdered) just inland at Reykholt, close to attractive waterfalls and more saga lore around Laxárdalur. Northwest of Borgarnes, the Snæfellsnes peninsula is dotted with fishing villages and its tip graced by Snæfellsjökull, the conical icecap covering a dormant volcano.

Búðir church

WEST ICELAND AND THE SNÆFELLSNES PENINSULA

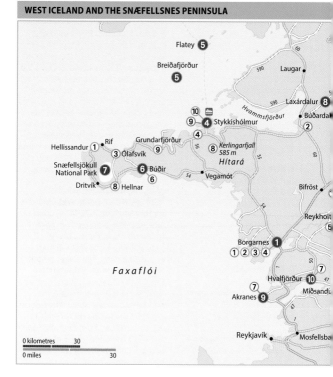

① Borgarnes Settlement Center

MAP B4 ■ Brákarbraut 13–15, Borgarnes ■ 437 1600 ■ Daily buses from Reykjavík to N1 in Borgarnes ■ Open 10am–9pm daily ■ Adm ■ www.landnam.is

These exhibitions *(see p42)* explore the Saga of the Settlement Period (AD 870–930) of Iceland, which began with Viking settlers and ended when all free land was taken. A section celebrates Iceland's most famous viking and first poet Egill Skallagrímsson.

② Hraunfossar, Barnafoss and Kaldidalur

MAP C4

About 15 km (9 miles) east up the valley from Reykholt on Route 518, the waterfalls at Hraunfossar and Barnafoss *(see p44)* – one gentle, the other violent – are worth a stop en route to Kaldidalur, a stark valley between the icy Ok and Þórisjökull peaks. The road is unsealed, but open in summer to ordinary vehicles (check conditions at www.vegagerdin.is).

Hraunfossar and Barnafoss waterfalls

③ Reykholt

MAP C4 ■ Snorrastofa, Reykholt ■ 433 8000 ■ Open May–Aug: 10am–5pm daily; Sep–Apr: 10am–5pm Mon–Fri; also open by request ■ Adm ■ www.snorrastofa.is

The tiny hamlet of Reykholt belies its importance as the home of Snorri Sturluson (1179–1241), the historian who became tangled in Norway's bid to annex Iceland. Murdered by a rival with the support of the Norwegian king Hákon (he was trapped and killed in the cellar of his own house), his tale is told at the cultural and medieval centre Snorrastofa. His thermal bathing pool and the restored remains of the tunnel which once led there from his home are located nearby.

④ Stykkishólmur

MAP B3 ■ www.stykkisholmur.is ■ Norska Húsið: 433 8114; open Jun–Aug: 11am–5pm daily; adm; www.norskahusid.is ■ Library of Water: 865 4516; open Jul & Aug: 11am–5pm daily, Sep–May: 1–4pm Tue–Sat; adm; www.vatnasafn.is

This town's wooden buildings recall its 19th-century port heyday, the best being Norska Húsið (Norwegian House). The nearby countryside is dotted with sites from *Eyrbyggja Saga* *(see p86)*. The Library of Water has 24 glass columns filled with water from Iceland's major glaciers.

Hvammstángi

Vatnsdalsá

Brú

Norðurá

35

Arnarvatnsheiði

⑥ Hraunfossar and Barnafoss
② Barnafoss
⑤ Húsafell

Langjökull

Ok △
0 m

② Kaldidalur

Skorradalsvatn

garvatn.

gvallavatn

①	**Top 10 Sights** *see pp83–5*
①	**Places to Eat** *see p87*
①	**The Best of the Rest** *see p86*

Snæfellsjökull, the icecapped volcano at the centre of the national park

5 Breiðafjörður and Flatey
MAP B3 ■ Sea Tours: www.sea
tours.is ■ Flatey: www.hotelflatey.is

Breiðafjörður – the huge, wide
bay separating the Snæfellsnes
peninsula from the Westfjords to
the north – is thick with islands
and rocky reefs, providing an ideal
breeding ground for marine birds.
From Stykkishólmur, you can
explore the bay on a tour with Sea
Tours (see p71), or go to Brjánslækur
in the Westfjords via Breiðafjörður's
largest island, Flatey, once home to
an important monastery. For a taste
of island life and bird-watching,
stay in Flatey's tiny village.

6 Búðir
MAP A4

Búðir is a minute place on the south
coast of Snæfellsnes, with just a
church and a hotel. One can enjoy
beautiful seascapes and views of
Snæfellsjökull (see pp26–7) from
here. The dark wooden church dates
from 1703. Its graveyard and bound-
aries are encroached upon by the
Búðahraun lava field, which is said to
be inhabited by creatures from local
folklore. Despite its remote location,
the romantic Hótel Búðir (see p130)
is famous for being a favourite of
Nobel Prize-winning author Halldór
Laxness. Don't miss the amazing
black-sand beach.

7 Snæfellsjökull National Park

Based around an icecapped
volcano, this national park (see
pp26–7) extends over rough, vegetated lava fields to a coastline
rich in birdlife. You can hike here,
explore local villages near the
glacier or visit Vatnshellir lava
cave – although using a guide is
recommended for all. You can
circuit the park by car in a day.

8 Laxárdalur
MAP C3

This valley along Route 59 is
the setting for *Laxdæla Saga*, the
great tragic love story of Icelandic
literature. It tells of the beautiful
Guðrún Ósvífursdóttir and her four
husbands: the first she divorces, but
the rest perish due to witchcraft,
feuding and drowning, respectively,

EGIL'S SAGA

An interesting mixture of history,
folklore and political allegory, *Egil's
Saga* recounts the roller-coaster life of
Egill Skallagrímsson (AD 910–990), a
bully of a Viking who spent his youth
fighting the Norwegians and his old
age fighting everyone else, but was
nonetheless a magnificent poet. A
must-read, along with *Njál's Saga* and
Laxdæla Saga.

while she becomes a nun. Only place names from that time survive, namely the church at Hjarðarholt, and the farmsteads at Goddastaðir and Höskuldsstaðir.

9 Akranes
MAP B5

Akranes, Iceland's oldest fishing port, is a good place to experience a down-to-earth, gritty Icelandic town. Fishing is still the main industry and the town is famous for its sports club, Íþróttabandalag Akranes, whose football team has won the Icelandic Championship 18 times. The engaging Akranes Folk Museum (see p86) and a charming lighthouse provide good reasons to visit this town, though their location is a 10-km (6-mile) detour off the highway.

10 Hvalfjörður
MAP C4

Most people use the tunnel under the bay to bypass the 30-km- (19-mile-) deep Hvalfjörður and miss some classic scenery, including Glymur (see p44), Iceland's highest waterfall. Hvalfjörður means "whale fjord", after the number of whales once seen here. It was a US naval base during World War II and the red barracks are now holiday homes.

Glymur waterfall

See map on pp82–3 ←

A DAY IN THE WEST

▶ MORNING

Drive north from Reykjavík around Kjalarnes, where the road nips between the sea and the Esja plateau. Avoid the 6-km- (4-mile-) long cross-fjord tunnel and follow Route 47 around **Hvalfjörður**. At the head of the fjord, take the 4-km (3-mile) gravel road inland, and then hike 5.5-km (3.5-mile), to where the Glymur waterfall cascades down the 200-m- (656-ft-) high cliffs. Continue around Hvalfjörður to rejoin Route 1 and continue to **Borgarnes** (see p83). Spend an hour at the Settlement Center, delving into the lives of Iceland's Viking pioneers. Don't miss out on the spooky dioramas downstairs, retelling the tale of Egil's Saga. Have a quick lunch at the good-value café here.

AFTERNOON

Make **Deildartunguhver** (see p48), Europe's largest thermal spring, the first stop of the afternoon, followed by a further historical halt at **Reykholt** (see p83), taking in the Heimskringla Museum, the church and old geothermal bathing pool. From here, follow Route 518 to **Hraunfossar** and **Barnafoss** (see p44), the latter is the setting for a tragic tale of two children who drowned in the rapids here while trying to cross over a lava bridge. Both falls are small but attractive. At this point you can retrace your route or (though this is an adventurous, summer-only option) follow gravel tracks south via **Kaldidalur** (see p83) to **Þingvellir** (see pp12–13) and then back to Reykjavík.

The Best of the Rest

1 Borg á Mýrum
MAP B4

Site of Egill Skallagrímsson's home, but nothing contemporary is left. The statue *Sonatorrek (Lament for my Dead Son)* is named after his poem.

Sonatorrek

2 Eiríksstaðir
MAP C3

■ Eiríksstaðir, Haukadal, 371 Búðardalur ■ 899 7111 ■ Open May–Sep: 10am–4pm daily ■ Adm ■ www.eiriksstadir.is

Reconstructed longhouse of Viking Eiríkr Þorvaldsson, known as Eirik the Red, and his son Leifur, who explored Greenland and North America.

3 Pakkhúsið
MAP A3 ■ Ólafsbraut, Ólafsvík ■ 857 5050 ■ Open summer: noon–5pm daily; winter: by appointment ■ Adm

This 1844 warehouse houses a folk museum and a store, Útgerðin. Photographs and fishing memorabilia outline the town's history.

4 Berserkjahraun
MAP B3

Eyrbyggja Saga tells how a warrior was promised a local man's daughter if he cleared a path through this lava field, but was murdered once he completed the task.

5 Húsafell
MAP C4

Picturesque spread of woodland and meadows east of Reykholt, with an old church, open-air geothermal swimming pool and petrol station serving the scattered community of summer houses used by holiday-makers. Home to artist Páll Guðmundsson.

6 Víðgelmir Cave
MAP C4 ■ 783 3600
■ www.thecave.is

Iceland's largest and grandest lava cave, which features spectacular colours and lava formations.

7 Akranes Folk Museum
MAP B5 ■ Garðaholt 3, Akranes ■ 433 1150 ■ Open mid-May–mid-Sep: 10am–5pm daily; mid-Sep–mid-May: by appointment ■ Adm ■ www. museum.is

This museum looks at the past living conditions of people in the area.

8 Kerlingarfjall
MAP B3

Route 56 to Stykkishólmur crosses Kerlingarfjall, a mountain said to be haunted by the ghost of a female troll, who turned to stone on her way back from a fishing expedition.

9 Stykkishólmur Church
MAP B3 ■ Open 10am–5pm daily ■ Adm for recitals

Shaped like an abstract ship, the church holds music recitals from June to August.

10 Glanni
MAP C4

A pretty cascade over black lava on the Norðurá salmon river near Bifröst. You can see salmon swim upstream.

Berserkjahraun lava field

Places to Eat

PRICE CATEGORIES
For a three-course meal for one with half a bottle of wine (or equivalent meal), including taxes and extra charges.
....
Ⓚ under ISK5,000   ⓀⓀ ISK5,000–9,000
ⓀⓀⓀ over ISK9,000

Hótel Búðir

① Viðvík
MAP A3 ▪ Hellissandur 360
▪ 436 1026 ▪ ⓀⓀ

Set against the spectacular views of the Snæfellsjökull glacier and the ocean, Viðvík has a top-notch menu that is updated seasonally. Try the langoustine bisque and cod dishes.

② Hótel Hamar
MAP B4 ▪ Ⓚ

Not the most formal of fine dining restaurants, Hótel Hamar *(see p130)* offers a gourmet menu that includes the catch-of-the-day. The restaurant has beautiful views of Borgarfjörður fjord.

③ Settlement Center
MAP B4 ▪ Brákarbraut 13–15, Borgarnes ▪ 437 1600 ▪ Ⓚ

Great for an inexpensive meal – you can choose from the extensive à la carte menu or the lunch buffet, which has a variety of salads, pasta and freshly baked bread.

④ N1
MAP B4 ▪ Brúartorg, Borgarnes ▪ Ⓚ

An alternative to the ever-crowded N1 petrol station canteen – known by the same name – N1 is a good place to grab a quick sandwich or a pizza during the day.

⑤ Fosshótel Reykholt
MAP C4 ▪ 320 Reykholt ▪ 435 1260 ▪ www.fosshotel.is ▪ Ⓚ

A top choice in Reykholt – the restaurant in this hotel offers dishes such as slow cooked lamb with red cabbage and pasta tagliatelle with roasted nuts. The desserts are top-notch, too.

⑥ Hótel Búðir
MAP A4 ▪ ⓀⓀ

The restaurant in Hotel Búðir *(see p130)*, serves fresh lamb and seafood dishes in a smart setting. European wine pairings are also available.

⑦ Hótel Glymur
MAP C3 ▪ Hvalfjörður ▪ 430 3100 ▪ www.hotelglymur.is ▪ Ⓚ

Smart retreat with an accomplished menu – carpaccio beef, pan-seared trout and homemade ice cream. The café serves tasty snacks.

⑧ Fjöruhúsið
MAP A4 ▪ Hellnar, Snæfellsnes ▪ 435 6844 ▪ Closed Dec–May ▪ Ⓚ

A small café with good-value meals. it is famous for fish soup, coffee, cakes and harbour views.

⑨ Bjargarsteinn
MAP B3 ▪ Sólvellir 15, Grundarfjörður ▪ 438 6770 ▪ Closed L ▪ www.bjargarsteinn.is ▪ Ⓚ

This is a cosy family-owned restaurant overlooking the Kirkjufell mountain. They offer both traditional and contemporary dishes such as the fish of the day which is popular. Local and seasonal ingredients are used whenever possible.

⑩ Narfeyrarstofa
MAP B3 ▪ Aðalgata 3, Stykkishólmur ▪ 438 1119 ▪ www.narfeyrarstofa.is ▪ ⓀⓀ

Narfeyrarstofa is set in an old wooden building with a tiny lounge. Try the scallops from Breiðarfjörður Bay, pan-fried in butter, garlic and chili, served with Icelandic barley.

See map on pp82–3 ⟵

🔟 The Westfjords

There is grandeur in the high mountains, blue seas and rugged coastline of the Westfjords, located in the extreme northwest of Iceland. For the region's scattered communities, life has been tough given the minimal infrastructure outside Ísafjörður, the only sizable town. The attractions of the area are mostly strung along the west coast between the Látrabjarg Bird Cliffs and Ísafjörður. Though the eastern Strandir coast offers a low-key beauty, inland views are filled by snow-streaked plateaus. The area is best visited in summer when the roads are open and you can drive here or take a bus from Reykjavík. You can also fly into places like Ísafjörður, and use buses or a car to get around.

Thermal pool, Flókalundur

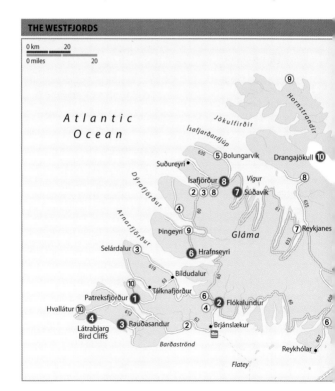

THE WESTFJORDS

0 km   20
0 miles   20

Atlantic Ocean

Jökulfirðir

Ísafjarðardjúp

Hornstrandir

⑨

630 ⑤ Bolungarvík

Drangajökull ⑩

Suðureyri •

Ísafjörður ⑧
② ③ ⑧

Vigur

⑧

⑦ Súðavík

Dýrafjörður

④

⑦ Reykjanes

Þingeyri ⑨

Gláma

613 635

Arnarfjörður

Selárdalur ③

⑥ Hrafnseyri

619

Bíldudalur

60

⑩

63

• Tálknafjörður

Patreksfjörður ①

⑥ ② Flókalundur

Hvallátur ⑩

613

④

② 62

• Brjánslækur

608

⑥

④
Látrabjarg
Bird Cliffs

③ Rauðasandur

Barðaströnd

607

Reykhólar •

Flatey

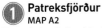
Wild flowers near Patreksfjörður

1 Patreksfjörður
MAP A2

Named after St Patrick, this sizable fishing village on Route 62 is where Iceland's trawling industry started in the early 20th century. It is famous for attacks by Basque whalers during the early 17th century. It is also the last place to stock up with provisions and fuel if you are heading to the Látrabjarg bird cliffs or the beach at Breiðavík (see pp28–9), which is southwest on Route 612.

1 **Top 10 Sights**
see pp89–91

1 **Places to Eat**
see p93

1 **The Best of the Rest**
see p92

2 Flókalundur
MAP B2 ■ Vatnsfjörður Nature Reserve: www.ust.is

Flókalundur ("Flóki's Wood") is a tiny south-coast area on Route 62, named after the Viking Flóki Vilgerðarson. He endured a harsh winter here around AD 860 and, on climbing nearby Lómfell, he saw the fjord below choked with ice and gave "Ice Land" its name. The surrounding wetlands, dwarf forest and barren basalt highlands are now protected as the Vatnsfjörður Nature Reserve. You can explore it using Hótel Flókalundur (see p93) as a summertime base.

3 Rauðasandur
MAP A3

Seals are frequently seen at this cinnamon-coloured beach on the southwesternmost peninsula of the Westfjords, along the unsealed Route 614. Arctic skuas nest on the grasslands behind the spit. As well as offering wildlife, the ruins of Sjöundá farm lie 5 km (3 miles) east of the beach. Gunnar Gunnarsson's novel Svartfugl (Blackbird) is based on a double murder there in 1802.

4 Látrabjarg Bird Cliffs

This is among the most stirring sights in Iceland (see pp28–9). Millions of seabirds cram into the cliffs in summer – the noise and stench are remarkable. The dramatic landscape, empty beaches and isolated buildings evoke the hardships of rural life. Local buses travel here in summer.

The dramatic Látrabjarg Bird Cliffs

5 Hólmavík Museum of Sorcery and Witchcraft

MAP C2 ▪ Höfðagata 8, 510 Hólmavík ▪ 897 6525 ▪ Summer: open 10am–6pm daily; winter: open 12am–6pm Mon–Fri, 1–6pm Sat & Sun ▪ Adm ▪ www.galdrasyning.is

Set on the east coast of the Westfjords, Hólmavík Museum of Sorcery and Witchcraft draws on the district's reputation for the dark arts – during the 17th century 20 people (only one was female) were burned at the stake. The museum has models and trinkets and also runs a "Sorcerer's Cottage" 28 km (17 miles) up the coast, which shows how people lived in the 17th century. Grab a bite at the restaurant, Galdur.

6 Hrafnseyri

MAP B2 ▪ 456 8260 ▪ Open Jun–8 Sep: 11am–6pm daily ▪ www.hrafnseyri.is

This spot is the birthplace of Jón Sigurðsson (1811–79), who campaigned for Iceland's independence from Denmark. Today, Hrafnseyri is home to a museum, with a fascinating exhibition all about Sigurðsson's life. Next door is a turf farmhouse (also part of the museum), which is a replica of his home; it contains a small café that serves delicious coffee and cakes. Also close by is a small church, dating back to 1886. Don't miss the Dynjandi waterfall located 22 km (14 miles) to the south.

TIMBER FROM THE SEA

Iceland has always been short of home-grown timber for building boats and houses, which has from Viking times has placed great demand on driftwood. Fortunately, plenty washes up around the country, particularly along the Westfjords' pebbly Strandir coast, whose beaches are often strewn with tree trunks that have floated all the way from Siberia.

7 Súðavík Arctic Fox Centre

MAP B2 ▪ Eyrardal, Súðavík ▪ 456 4922 ▪ Open May & Sep: 9am–3:30pm daily (Jun–Aug: to 6pm) ▪ Adm ▪ www.arcticfoxcenter.com

Originally the only mammal to inhabit Iceland was the Arctic fox, which probably drifted here from Greenland on ice floes. Smaller than the European red fox, the Arctic fox can either have a brown coat all year, or a grey one in summers and white in winters. The Arctic Fox Centre, located at Eyrardalur farm, 20 km (12 miles) around the coast from Ísafjörður, explores the animal's biology and relationship with humans. Rescued foxes can be found in the centre's garden.

Hikers admiring the Dynjandi waterfall, south of Hrafnseyri

8 Ísafjörður

MAP B2 ▪ Tourist office: 450 8060; www.isafjordur.is ▪ Westfjords Maritime Museum: Turnhús, Suðurgata, Ísafjörður; 456 3291; open late May–late Aug: 10am–5pm daily; adm; www.nedsti.is

The region's main town, Ísafjörður is a mass of narrow streets and old buildings. Chief among these is the Turnhús, which houses the Westfjords Maritime Museum (see p43). Across the Ísafjarðardjúp straits, the uninhabited Hornstrandir peninsula offers the ultimate hiking challenge. Boats run out here and to little Vigur island (see p70) through the summer.

Traditional buildings, Ísafjörður

9 Norðurfjörður

MAP C2

At the end of Route 643 up the east Strandir coast, Norðurfjörður is small, even for the Westfjords, but the scenery is stunning and makes the drive along gravel roads worthwhile. The town is backed by the 646-m- (2,125-ft-) high Krossnesfjall hill and looks out to the sea across Norðurfjörður bay. About 4 km (2 miles) away lies Krossneslaug, a beachside swimming pool fed by a hot spring.

10 Drangajökull

MAP B2

The area's sole permanent icecap sits atop a high plateau. During the 18th century it covered local farms but has now shrunk. The dead-end Route 635 leads up to Kaldalón (see p92), a tiny fjord offering views of Drangajökull. From here it's an hour's walk towards Kaldalónsjökull, a glacier descending off the larger icecap.

A DAY IN THE WESTFJORDS

▶ **MORNING**

Arriving at **Brjánslækur** by ferry from Stykkishólmur on the Snæfellsnes peninsula (see p83), drive north up Route 62 to **Flókalundur** (see p89). Fuel up and buy something for a picnic lunch here before turning onto Route 60. This good gravel road climbs up to the Dynjandisheiði plateau and then drops abruptly to the coast at the stunning and noisy **Dynjandi** waterfall (see p45), a great place to stretch your legs and spend an hour exploring the multilevel cascades (the lighting is best here in the evening). A grassy area at the foot of the falls makes a perfect spot for a picnic.

AFTERNOON

Leaving Dynjandi waterfall, carry on around the bay to **Hrafnseyri**, birthplace of Jón Sigurðsson (see p37), and drop in at the museum celebrating the life of this great Icelandic patriot. From here it is a further 65 km (40 miles) to **Ísafjörður** via Þingeyri (the Westfjords' oldest trading town), two mountain passes and a lengthy single-lane tunnel – there are passing bays inside, but traffic is never heavy. Once at Ísafjörður, track down your accommodation and then visit the **Westfjords Maritime Museum** (see p43) inside the old Turnhús or simply stroll down to the harbour, where you can usually spot marine ducks. The nearby **Hotel Ísafjörður** (see p93) is an ideal place for enjoying a hearty evening meal.

See map on pp88–9 ←

The Best of the Rest

Djúpavík's rugged coastline

1 Djúpavík
MAP C2

Wild, beautiful Djúpavík, halfway along Strandir's coast, is dominated by a century-old shipwreck and a former herring processing factory that hosts exhibitions in the summer.

2 Reiðskörð
MAP A3

Route 62 runs past this tall and fragmented volcanic dyke at Barðaströnd, the bay south of the Westfjords.

3 Selárdalur
MAP A2 ■ Arnarfjörður

Self-taught artist Samúel Jónsson (1884–1969) lived in this isolated valley at the end of Route 619, and left behind a bizarre range of sculptures and buildings.

4 Skrúður
MAP A2 ■ Núpur

Set at the foot of a valley on Route 624, Iceland's oldest botanic garden was founded as a teaching garden in 1909 by Reverend Sigtryggur Guðlaugsson.

5 Bolungarvík
MAP B1 ■ Ósvör Maritime Museum: 892 5744, 456 7005; open by appointment; www.osvor.is

This fishing port is the second-largest town in the Westfjords. As well as offering some decent local hiking opportunities, the town is home to the Ósvör Maritime Museum, which exhibits a replica of a traditional Icelandic fishing boat.

6 Pennugil
MAP B2

This narrow canyon on the Penná river is about a 30-minute walk from Flókalundur. There is a hot spring feeding the river, suitable for bathing.

7 Reykjanes
MAP B2

The hamlet of Reykjanes has a geothermal pool and sauna.

8 Kaldalón
MAP B2

Kaldalón ("Cold Lagoon") is fed by Drangajökull glacier (see p91). It inspired local musician Sigvaldi Stefánsson (1881–1946) to call himself Kaldalóns.

9 Hælavíkurbjarg
MAP B1

This vertical 258-m- (847-ft-) high cliff between Hælavík and Hornvík islets is only accessible by boat. It is one of the area's major bird colonies, along with Látrabjarg and Hornbjarg.

10 Hvallátur
MAP A2 ■ www.breidavik.is

Iceland's westernmost settlement (see p29) comprises a farm and hotel at Breiðavík beach. It played a central role in the *Dhoon* shipwreck rescue (see p29) in 1947.

Places to Eat

PRICE CATEGORIES

For a three-course meal for one with half a bottle of wine (or equivalent meal), including taxes and extra charges.

Ⓚ under ISK5,000 　ⒺⓀ ISK5,000–9,000
ⓀⓀⓀ over ISK9,000

1 Hótel Djúpavík
MAP C2 ■ Djúpavík, Strandir
■ 451 4037 ■ www.djupavik.com ■ ⓀⓀ

Friendly, and with a fantastic location, this hotel serves tasty, home-cooked food in a cosy, wood-beamed dining room. Try the pan-fried cod served with rice and salad.

2 Einarshúsið
MAP B1 ■ Hafnargötu 41, Bolungarvík ■ 456 7901 ■ ⓀⓀ

Located in the small fishing village of Bolungarvík, this restaurant is set in a charming historic building. The place specializes in Icelandic seafood dishes, including an evening buffet with a variety of fresh fish caught from the local harbour.

3 Hamraborg Snack Bar
MAP B2 ■ Hafnarstræti 7, Ísafjörður ■ 456 3166 ■ Ⓚ

This fast-food place serves burgers, sandwiches, pizza and *pylsur* (hot dogs) with a variety of toppings including remoulade, onions and tomato sauce.

4 Hótel Flókalundur
This small hotel-restaurant offers lunch specials (including a meal of the day), smaller meals and a dinner menu that features local game and seafood. Wines and beers are also available.

5 Hótel Laugarhóll
MAP B3 ■ Strandir, Bjarnarfjörður ■ 451 3380
■ www.laugarholl.is ■ ⓀⓀ

Pleasant hotel in a marvellous setting with a thermal pool and hiking trails within walking distance. Its excellent restaurant has set menus.

6 Hótel Bjarkalundur
MAP B3 ■ Reykhólahreppi
■ 894 1295 ■ ⓀⓀ

This welcoming restaurant serves traditional Icelandic dishes made from fresh local ingredients.

7 Café Riis
MAP C2 ■ Hafnarbraut 39, Hólmavík ■ 451 3567 ■ Closed Sep–May ■ Ⓚ

The best restaurant on the Strandir coast, serving pan-fried chicken breast, roast trout and lamb fillets. Also offers pizzas, burgers and cakes.

8 Hótel Ísafjörður
MAP B2 ■ 456 3360 ■ ⓀⓀ

The hotel-restaurant *(see p130)*, Við Pollinn, has Nordic decor and offers tasty local fare such as catch of the day, grilled lamb and seafood soup.

Dining room at Hótel Ísafjörður

9 Simbahöllin
MAP B2 ■ Fjarðargata 5, 470 Þingeyri ■ 899 6659 ■ Closed Oct–May
■ www.simbahollin.is ■ Ⓚ

Charming café set inside an old wooden grocery store, with excellent coffee, soups, stews and a local take on Belgian waffles. The owners offer horse-riding tours and rent out bikes.

10 Tjöruhúsið
MAP B2 ■ Neðstakaupstað, 400 Ísafjörður ■ 456 4419 ■ ⓀⓀ

Set on Ísafjörður's waterfront, Tjöruhúsið *(see pp62–3)* is an excellent seafood restaurant. They don't go by a specific menu and usually serve the catch-of-the-day. Children under 14 can dine here for free.

See map on pp88–9 ←

TOP 10 North Iceland

North Iceland could easily make for a week-long trip all on its own with its landscapes and rich wildlife. There is Akureyri, the capital city, with its fjord setting and old buildings, and the sea-side town of Húsavík, known for its laid-back charm, unusual museums and whale-watching cruises. Natural beauty is also found here thanks to the dramatic canyon Jökulsárgljúfur, endless waterfalls and the volcanic Lake Mývatn. Added to this are a wealth of antique farms, churches and saga sites – such as Hólar – all of which make this region significant in terms of Icelandic history and culture. Most sights in this region are located on, or easy to reach from, Route 1, making it very accessible. Take the Arctic Coast Way to discover the most remote places.

Beautiful Rauðhólar

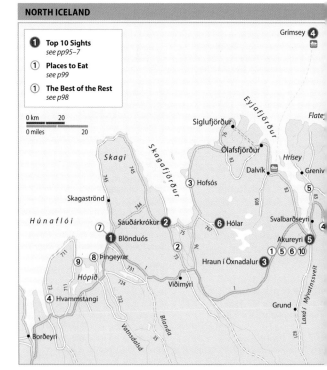

NORTH ICELAND

1. **Top 10 Sights**
   see pp95–7

① **Places to Eat**
   see p99

① **The Best of the Rest**
   see p98

0 km   20
0 miles   20

Grímsey ❹

Siglufjörður

Ólafsfjörður

Eyjafjörður

Flate

Hrísey

Dalvík

Greniv ❺

Skagi

Skagafjörður

③ Hofsós

Svalbarðseyri

Skagaströnd

Saúðárkrókur ❷

❻ Hólar

Akureyri ❺

Húnaflói

⑦

❶ Blönduós

① ❺ ❻ ❿ ⑩

⑧ Þingeyrar

Laxá Mývatnssveit

⑨

Hraun í Öxnadalur ❸

Hópið

Viðimýri

Grund

④ Hvammstangi

Blanda

Borðeyri

Vatnsdalsá

Atmospheric old buildings, Sauðárkrókur town square

① Blönduós
MAP D2

This port has a striking church, with steeply sloping concrete walls echoing the shape of the mountains. Other attractions include trips to see seals and birdlife in the bay and, 15 km (9 miles) west at Vatnsdalshólar, an expanse of mounds formed during an earthquake is the site of Iceland's last execution in 1830.

② Sauðárkrókur
MAP D2 ■ Drangey boat trips with Viggó Jónsson: 821 0090; open May–Aug: www.drangey.net

The appeal of Sauðárkrókur comes from the old buildings that surround the town square, principally the church and Hótel Tindastóll (see p133), which are said to be haunted. The coast here features in *Grettir's Saga*: Grettislaug, a seaside thermal bathing pool, is where he recovered after swimming over from Drangey island (see p71) in search of fresh embers to reignite his own fire.

③ Hraun í Öxnadalur
MAP E2

This farm in the deep Öxnadalur valley is famous as the birth-place of poet and biologist Jónas Hallgrímsson (1807–45). His romantic verses extolling the landscape influenced Icelanders – most of whom then lived in poverty in rural turf buildings – to begin to perceive their country as glorious, rather than embarrassing.

④ Grímsey
MAP E1 ■ Flights from Akureyri Jun: daily; Jul–Aug: four times a week; rest of the year: three times a week ■ Ferry from Dalvík mid-Jan–May & Sep: four times a week; Jun–Aug: five times a week ■ www.grimsey.is/en

The only part of Iceland inside the Arctic Circle (see p71), Grímsey is 40 km (25 miles) north of the mainland, and is little more than 3 km (2 miles) long, with tiny Sandvík in the south being the only settlement. In the north, its sheer cliffs are packed with nesting seabirds in summer.

Raufarhöfn

Melrakkaslétta

Kópasker

Öxarfjörður

⑩

⑦ Húsavík

⑩ Jökulsárgljúfur

⑥

Krafla
818 m

⑨ Dettifoss

Grímsstaðir

⑦

Lake
Mývatn   ⑧ ② Reykjahlíð

③   *Hverfjall*
463 m

Jökulsá á Fjöllum

Skjálfandafljót

Ódáðahraun

Herðubreið
1,682 m

5 Akureyri

MAP E2 ■ Akureyrarkirkja: við Eyrarlandsveg 600; www. akureyrarkirkja.is

Iceland's largest settlement after Reykjavík, with a population of over 19,000, Akureyri is a relaxed town with a pretty harbour, shops, cafés and restaurants. Looming over everything is Akureyrarkirkja, a picturesque church, with stained-glass windows and modern depictions of famous Icelanders. Don't miss the Botanic Gardens, where both native and imported plants thrive, Akureyri Swimming Pool, with its geothermal heated water and hot tubs, or Akureyri Art Museum in the town centre.

Akureyrarkirkja's stained-glass windows

6 Hólar

MAP D2 ■ Tourist office: 455 6333; open Jun–Aug: 10am–10pm daily ■ www.visitholar.is

More fully known as Hólar í Hjaltadal, this was once the largest settlement in northern Iceland thanks to the monastery and religious school founded in 1106 by bishop Jón Ögmundsson,

GRETTIR'S SAGA

Grettir's Saga recounts the life of Grettir Ásmundarson, a fierce warrior who performs great deeds in the service of others, but is haunted by a *draugur*, or evil ghost. Grettir ends his life as an outlaw on Drangey island *(see p71)*, where he is finally killed by his enemies.

which attracted scholars and monks from across Europe. These institutions survived the Reformation – which saw the execution of Hólar's last Catholic bishop, Jón Arason – and today the cathedral *(see p39)* and the college specializing in aquaculture, rural tourism and horse science are among a handful of buildings found here.

7 Húsavík

MAP E2 ■ Whale-watching tours: www.salkawhalewatching.is, www.gentlegiants.is and www. northsailing.is ■ Whale Museum: Hafnarstétt 1, Húsavík; 414 2800; opening times vary, check website for details; adm; www.whalemuseum.is

Húsavík is Iceland's whale-watching capital. There are daily tours between March and December. Do not miss the superb Whale Museum. The coast offers good walks along headlands and little beaches from where you might see seals. Húsavík featured as the hometown of Eurovision hopefuls Lars and Sigrit in the film *Eurovision Song Contest: The Story of Fire Saga (2020)*.

A whale off the coast of Húsavík

8 Lake Mývatn

Whether you have come to this country to climb cinder cones, hike your way over steaming expanses of solidified lava, bathe in open-air geothermal pools, see hot mud pools, make a day-trip into the stark Interior deserts or simply to spend some time bird-watching, you will find it all at Lake Mývatn (see pp20–21). Although many of the sights are located around the lakeshore, you will need a vehicle in order to reach the outlying attractions, which include a flooded volcano crater known as "Hell".

Dettifoss waterfall

9 Dettifoss
MAP F2

One of Iceland's most spectacular waterfalls, the thundering cascades of Dettifoss are a testament to the power of nature. Two more water-falls are found nearby: upstream lies the smaller but no less specta-cular Selfoss, while downstream sits Hafragilsfoss, a splendid waterfall with a viewpoint inside the Jökulsárgljúfur canyon.

10 Jökulsárgljúfur
MAP F2

Set in a northern segment of the massive Vatnajökull National Park (see pp24–5), this mighty canyon is excellent for hiking, following the top of the gorge or cutting across a land rich in flowers and birdlife. Sights along the way include striking red formations at Rauðhólar, twisted hexagonal basalt columns at Hljóðaklettar, Hólmatungur's springs and Dettifoss (see p44).

A DAY IN THE LAKE MÝVATN AREA

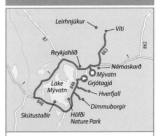

▶ **MORNING**

Start early, and you can just about pack all of the attractions of **Lake Mývatn** (see pp20–21) into one long summer day. Begin with the subterranean hot pools at Grjótagjá, then move south to tackle **Hverfjall**'s (see p21) slippery black slopes, making a circuit of the rim for spectacular views of the whole Mývatn area. Back at ground level, **Dimmuborgir** (see p20) presents an extraordinary maze of natural lava sculptures (look for rare gyrfalcons nesting on rocky towers here), with only a short drive to the lakeshore at Höfði Nature Park, where you will definitely encounter numerous species of waterfowl, including barrow's goldeneye, scaup and merganser. Follow the road to the south side of the lake at Skútustaðir, home to a large group of grassy pseudocraters.

AFTERNOON

Depending on your progress, you can grab lunch at the Dimmuborgir or Skútustaðir cafés, or circuit the lake to Reykjahlíð's Gamli Bærinn. Head east to the fear-some **Námaskarð** (see p21) mud pits, set in a wasteland full of steam and eye-watering smells. A good side road runs north from here, via the Leirbotn Power Station, to where Víti volcano overlooks Leirhnjúkur, a huge expanse of steaming lava laid down in the 1980s – a place for careful exploration. Round off the day with a good soak on the way home at the ⬤ Mývatn Nature Baths (see p21).

See map on pp94–5 ←

The Best of the Rest

The gushing Goðafoss waterfall

1 Goðafoss

This waterfall *(see p45)* is named after events that occurred when Christianity came here in AD 1000.

2 Glaumbær

MAP D2 ■ Glaumbær, 561 Varmahlíð ■ 453 6173 ■ Open mid-May–mid-Sep: 9am–6pm daily; Apr–mid-May & mid-Sep–mid-Oct: 10am–4pm Mon–Fri (by request mid-Oct–Mar: Mon–Fri) ■ Adm ■ www.glaumbaer.is

A turf farmhouse, this was built between 1750 and 1879. The use of imported timber hints at the family's comparative wealth.

3 Hofsós

MAP C4

Visit the Icelandic Emigration Centre *(see p42)*, one of the country's oldest timber buildings *(Pakkhúsið)*, and have a dip in the pool *(see p53)*.

4 Vaglaskógur

MAP E2 ■ 462 4755 ■ Campsite: open May–Sep

This stretch of birch woodland along Fnjóskadalur valley is a popular camping area with a store and walking trails.

5 Laufás

MAP E2 ■ 463 3196 ■ Open May–Oct ■ Adm ■ www.minjasafnid.is

The heritage site and museum, housed in a 19th-century turf farmhouse, displays period household items. The town's church is also worth visiting for its 17th-century pulpit.

6 Grenjaðarstaður

MAP E2 ■ 464 3688 ■ Open Jun–Aug: 10am–6pm daily ■ Adm

Some buildings here have flowers on their turf roofs. Visit the cemetery to see headstones carved with runes.

7 Laxá í Aðaldal

Better known for its fishing potential further downstream, the Laxá's turbulent flow as it exits Lake Mývatn *(see p21)* is a magnet for red-necked phalarope, barrow's goldeneye and harlequin duck.

8 Þingeyrakirkja

MAP C2 ■ Þingeyrar, near Blönduós ■ 895 4473 ■ Open 10am–5pm Mon, Wed & Fri–Sun ■ Adm

Built between 1864 and 1977, this remarkable church *(see p39)* sits alone on a vegetated sandbar. A visitor centre next door runs guided tours.

9 Hvítserkur

MAP C2

This natural rock formation, which resembles a 15-m- (49-ft-) tall dinosaur drinking from the sea, lies on the east of the Vatnsnes peninsula on Route 711.

Hvítserkur rock formation

10 Tjörnes

MAP E2

This rounded peninsula with distinct banded geological strata yields bivalve and plant fossils. A signposted fossil bed is located near Ytri-Tunga farm.

Places to Eat

PRICE CATEGORIES

For a three-course meal for one with half a bottle of wine (or equivalent meal), including taxes and extra charges.

Ⓚ under ISK5,000 　⒦Ⓚ ISK5,000–9,000
⒦ⓀⓀ over ISK9,000

① Múlaberg Bistro & Bar
MAP E2 ▪ Hafnarstræti 87–89, 600 Akureyri ▪ 460 2000 ▪ ⓀⓀ

This bistro and bar in Hótel KEA (see p130) has a great selection of steaks and a buzzing cocktail bar.

② Gamli Bærinn
MAP F2 ▪ Reykjahlíð, Mývatn ▪ 464 4170 ▪ Closed Sep–Apr ▪ Ⓚ

This café-bar in the Hótel Mývatn serves beer, light meals, snacks, coffee and great lamb soup.

③ Vogafjos Café
MAP F2 ▪ Vogar, 660 Mývatn ▪ 464 3800 ▪ Opening hours vary during winter ▪ www.vogafjos.is

Set inside a cowshed (you can see the cows through a transparent wall), this café serves tasty meals and cheeses made from fresh cows' milk.

④ Sjavarborg Restaurant
MAP C3 ▪ Strandgata 1, Hvammstangi ▪ 451 3131 ▪ www.sjavarborg-restaurant.is ▪ ⓀⓀⓀ

Located on Hvammstangi's harbour, this restaurant offers a range of main courses, including fish soup and fresh fish.

⑤ Greifinn
MAP E2 ▪ Glerágata 20, Akureyri ▪ 460 1600 ▪ Ⓚ

A no-nonsense pizza restaurant, with an extensive menu. Takeaway options are available but it is also a lovely place to sit and eat.

⑥ Bláa Kannan
MAP E2 ▪ Hafnarstræti 96, Akureyri ▪ 461 4600 ▪ Ⓚ

With an unmistakable corrugated iron exterior painted dark blue, and tables spilling out onto the street, this is your best bet in town for coffee, cake and people-watching.

⑦ Hótel Blanda
MAP D2 ▪ Aðalgata 6, 540 Blönduós ▪ 452 4205 ▪ ⓀⓀ

The restaurant at this hotel offers lunch and dinner menus featuring a range of meat and fish dishes, the latter prepared with the catch-of-the-day.

⑧ Gamli Baukur
MAP E2 ▪ Harbour, Húsavík ▪ 464 2442 ▪ Ⓚ

Housed in wooden warehouses overlooking the harbour, this snug place serves soups and fresh fish daily, all at a reasonable cost, given the portions.

⑨ Salka
MAP E2 ▪ Garðarsbraut 6, Húsavík ▪ 464 2551 ▪ Ⓚ

Offering competition to nearby Gamli Baukur, this restaurant has a similar menu but with the bonus of plenty of outdoor tables to linger at when the sun is shining.

⑩ Bautinn
MAP E2 ▪ Hafnarstræti 92, Akureyri ▪ 462 1818 ▪ Ⓚ

This unpretentious restaurant has been in operation since 1971. It serves customers a selection of fresh fish, lamb, steaks and burgers.

Bautinn restaurant's exterior

See map on pp94–5

🔟 East Iceland

East Iceland covers a varied region of broad river valleys, boggy plateaus surrounding the Vatnajökull icecap, and a dramatic coastline forming the East Fjords. The main centres are Egilsstaðir, on the shores of Lagarfljót lake, and Höfn, a springboard for Vatnajökull National Park. Visiting smaller communities such as Vopnafjörður, Borgarfjörður Eystri and Seyðisfjörður provides insight into daily life here, while rewarding side trips include the Kárahnjúkar hydro dam.

Hallormsstaður forest

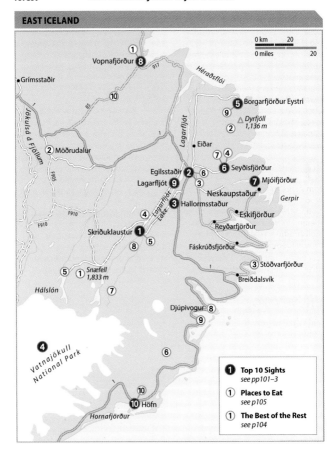

EAST ICELAND

1	Top 10 Sights *see pp101–3*
①	Places to Eat *see p105*
①	The Best of the Rest *see p104*

Skriðuklaustur

① Skriðuklaustur
MAP G3 ■ 471 2990 ■ Open Apr–May & Sep–Oct: 11am–5pm daily; Jun–Aug: 10am–6pm daily; Nov–Mar: times vary, call in advance ■ www.skriduklaustur.is

This villa belonging to author Gunnar Gunnarsson (1889–1975) sits on Lagarfljót's western shore, close to the church at Valþjófsstaður and Hengifoss. Gunnarsson's first novel, *Af Borgslægtens Historie*, was written here. The villa hosts exhibitions about the author and the ruins of a 16th-century monastery found nearby. Klausturkaffi café offers lunch and a buffet of homemade cakes. The Visitor Centre for Vatnajökull National Park is located nearby in a separate building.

② Egilsstaðir
MAP G3 ■ Summer-only buses from Akureyri and Reykjavík via Höfn; airport open year-round ■ East Iceland Heritage Museum: check website for opening times; www.minjasafn.is/english; adm ■ Wilderness Center: www.wilderness.is

Just east of Lagarfljót, Egilsstaðir's attractions include the East Iceland Heritage Museum, which features a *baðstofa* (the living room of a turf house), and the Wilderness Center – a guesthouse within a museum celebrating how Icelanders have survived in this difficult environment. The 70-km (44-mile) drive around Lagarfljót takes in saga sites, woodlands and one of Iceland's tallest waterfalls.

③ Hallormsstaður
MAP G3

Hallormsstaður sits beside Iceland's most extensive forest, grown since the 1900s for recreational use and for timber. A web of wooded walking trails heads up the valley slopes, while a roadside Forestry Office has a small arboretum with 40 tree species, including Iceland's tallest, a 22-m- (62-ft-) high larch.

④ Vatnajökull National Park
MAP F4

One of the largest in Europe, this national park extends all the way into South Iceland. The bulk of the park surrounds the Vatnajökull *(see pp24–5)* icecap, which stretches across a huge swathe of southern and eastern Iceland. In the vicinity of Skaftafell and Höfn, and easily accessible from the ring road, various glacier outlets crawl down to the lowland. Lakes have formed in front of most of these ice tongues making them quite picturesque. Snowmobile tours, glacier walks and other such activities are offered to the south of Vatnajökull.

Vatnajökull icecap, seen from Jökulsárlón lake

Borgafjörður Eystri settlement

5 Borgafjörður Eystri (Bakkagerði)
MAP H2

Part of the fun of visiting Borgafjörður Eystri, the East Fjords' most endearing settlement, is the journey via the Héraðsflói estuary's grassy lagoons and steep ranges that isolate the village. On arrival you will find a tiny community backed by the jagged Dyrfjöll mountain, with sights including a little hummock near the church named Álfaborg, home to Iceland's fairy queen (according to folklore), and a sizable puffin colony overlooking the fishing harbour. Superb, lengthy hiking trails lead south to Seyðisfjörður.

6 Seyðisfjörður
MAP H3

Seyðisfjörður's charm lies in its steep fjord setting and 19th-century wooden architecture near the harbour. The church, several houses and two hotels are the

pick, most painted in pastel hues and originally imported from Norway. An important naval station during World War II and a herring port before then, today Seyðisfjörður is linked to the Faroe Islands and Denmark by the *Norröna* ferry.

7 Mjóifjörður
MAP H3

A long, thin inlet accessed by the gravel Route 953, Mjóifjörður ("Narrow Fjord") is worth the bumpy drive to Brekka village and the remote lighthouse at Dalatangi. The road between the shoreline and steep mountains offers some close-ups of beautiful streams and cascades, plus the chance of seeing the Arctic fox, which is more at ease with humans in this remote area.

8 Vopnafjörður
MAP G2

If you are making the long coastal drive along Route 85 from Húsavík towards Egilsstaðir, set aside at least an hour for Vopnafjörður, a small town built on a steep prong of land. It has a museum detailing the plight of local communities following the 1875 eruption of Víti at Askja (see p47). An outdoor geothermal pool at Selárdalur and the immaculate collection of old turf farmhouses at Bustarfell (see p104) are located close by.

Nineteenth-century architecture, Seyðisfjörður

9 Lagarfljót
MAP G3

At 25 km (16 miles) long and – at its greatest width – 2.5 km (2 miles) wide, Lagarfljót (or Lögurinn) is a narrow sliver of a lake. Found to the west of Egilsstaðir *(see p101)*, its placid waters are rumoured to be home to a serpent-like monster known as the Lagarfljót Wyrm (Lagarfljotsormurinn).

Scenic view of Lagarfljót

10 Höfn
MAP G5 ■ Daily buses to Reykjavík and summer services to Egilsstaðir; airport open year-round

Höfn started life as a warehouse during the 1860s, and developed into a working port. It is a good base for trips to Vatnajökull National Park *(see pp24–5)*. The Glacier Exhibition fills you in on the area and you can book Skidoo trips and Jeep tours to the icecap. Hikers can aim for Lónsöræfi reserve. For glacier views, head for the landmark statue on the shore – avoiding the Arctic tern colony.

HÉRAÐSFLÓI'S BIRDLIFE

Héraðsflói – a broad bay with a black-sand beach and boggy meadows inland along the myriad of streamlets of the Jökulsá á Brú river – makes a superb place for observing birdlife. Look for marine ducks (including the long-tailed or old squaw and scoter), godwits, red-throated divers and even hobbys **(right)**, Iceland's smallest bird of prey.

A DAY IN EAST ICELAND

▶ MORNING

Before starting this 70-km (44-mile) circuit of Lagarfljót lake and the Lagarfljót valley, climb the hillock behind the Menntaskólinn school in **Egilsstaðir** *(see p101)* for a view of the region – on a clear day you can see as far as **Snæfell** *(see p104)*, Iceland's highest free-standing peak. Then head south, branching off the highway onto Route 931, past fields full of sheep and Icelandic horses, until a surprising amount of woodland begins to spring up around **Hallormsstaður** *(see p101)*, where you can explore walking tracks or the Forestry Office's arboretum, or take in lakeside views at Atlavík. Exiting the woods past Atlavík, the main road crosses the lake to Lagarfljót's west shore, where you turn left and drive some distance to **Skriðuklaustur** *(see p101)*.

AFTERNOON

After having a snack at Skriðuklaustur's café, Klausturkaffi, and visiting the National Park exhibition, continue south to **Valþjófsstaður** church *(see p104)* with its reproduction of carved Viking doors, then retrace your route back past Skriðuklaustur to where the 60-km- (37-mile-) long Route 910 ascends to moorlands around Snæfell and the **Kárahnjúkar Hydro Dam** *(see p104)*. You need 3 hours for this round trip, otherwise follow an hour-long walking track uphill to **Hengifoss** *(see p104)* after parking your car. Stay on the western shore for the drive back to Egilsstaðir.

See map on p100 ←

The Best of the Rest

1 Snæfell
MAP F4 ■ www.vatnajokulsth
jodgardur.is

This isolated, snowcapped basalt
core of an old volcano lies at
Vatnajökull's northeast corner. It is
located on a 4WD-only track. There
are hiking huts around the base.

2 Hvítserkur
MAP H3

A spectacular orange, pink and grey
rhyolite mountain 10 km (6 miles)
along a hiking trail from Borgafjörður
Eystri. The colours really stand
out after rain. The trail is straight-
forward, but be prepared for
changing weather.

3 Steinasafn Petru
MAP H4 ■ Fjarðarbraut 21,
755 Stöðvarfirði, East Fjords ■ 475
8834 ■ Open May–Sep/Oct:
9am–6pm daily ■ Adm

Extensive private geological collection,
featuring coloured stones, crystals
and mineral samples found in mainly
the eastern part of Iceland.

4 Hengifoss
MAP G3

This 118-m (387-ft) waterfall is
Iceland's highest, dropping in a
narrow ribbon off a cliff face layered in red and black. On the
way up, don't miss the twisted
basalt columns at Litlifoss.

5 Kárahnjúkar Hydro Dam
MAP F4

A controversial project that dammed
the Dimmugljúfur canyon in order
to provide power for a smelter. The
sealed road crosses highland tundra,
which is home to reindeer.

6 Lónsöræfi
MAP G4

This wild, uninhabited area is rich in
gorges, moorland and glacial scenery.
An unmarked, 5-day trail for self-
sufficient hikers runs from Stafafell
to Snæfell through this private reserve.

7 Eyjabakkar
MAP G4

Boggy highland region en route
to Kárahnjúkar or Snæfell, this is a
breeding ground for greylag geese
and whooper swans; reindeer
are common too.

8 Valþjófsstaður
MAP G3 ■ Open 10am–
5pm daily

Farm and red-roofed church, with
replica carved doors depicting a
knight slaying a dragon. The original
doors, dating from around AD 1200,
are in Reykjavík's National Museum.

9 Djúpivogur Bulandsnes
MAP G4 ■ www.djupivogur.is

Three beautiful fjords and a
profusion of Icelandic wildlife make
this area a nature-
lover's paradise.

10 Bustarfell
MAP G2 ■ 471
2211 ■ Open 1 Jun–20
Sep: 10am–5pm daily
■ Adm

Well-preserved
turf-roofed farm-
houses (rebuilt in
1770), occupied by
the same family since
1532. Café on site.

Hengifoss

Places to Eat

PRICE CATEGORIES
For a three-course meal for one with half
a bottle of wine (or equivalent meal),
including taxes and extra charges.

Ⓚ under ISK5,000   ⓀⓀ ISK5,000–9,000
ⓀⓀⓀ over ISK9,000

Nielsen Restaurant, Egilsstaðir

① Hótel Tangi
MAP G2 ∎ Hafnarbyggð 17,
Vopnafjörður ∎ 473 1203 ∎ ⓀⓀ

The hotel restaurant is the most
popular place to eat in Vopnafjörður,
and it's not hard to see why as their
pizzas and grilled fish are excellent.

② Fjallakaffi
MAP F3 ∎ Möðrudal á Fjöllum
∎ 471 1858, 894 0758 ∎ www.fjalla
dyrd.is ∎ Ⓚ

Attached to the highest farm in
Iceland (which offers accommodation),
this "café in the mountains" is reached
by Route 901, south off Route 1 from
Lake Mývatn. Fjallakaffi serves
traditional fare, including *kjötsúpa*
(lamb soup), *sláturterta* (lamb tart)
and *kleina* (an Icelandic doughnut).

③ Hérað – Berjaya Iceland Hotels
MAP G3 ∎ Miðvangur 5-7,
700 Egilsstaðir ∎ 471 1500 ∎ Ⓚ

Local reindeer steak is the obvious
dish to try at the restaurant in Hérað
(see p130). They also offer lamb and
seafood dishes.

④ Norð Austur
MAP H3 ∎ Norðurgata 2,
Seyðisfjörður ∎ Open 5–10pm Wed–
Sun ∎ www.nordaustur.is ∎ ⓀⓀⓀ

The menu features sushi, maki rolls
with Arctic char, salmon, cod, and
small plates such as lamb bulgogi
and tempura corn.

⑤ Klausturkaffi
MAP G3 ∎ Skriðuklaustur ∎ 471
2992 ∎ Open Apr–mid-Oct ∎ ⓀⓀ

This charming café serves Icelandic
staples as well as a delicious lunch
and cake buffet everyday in summer.

⑥ Nielsen Restaurant
MAP G3 ∎ Tjarnarbraut 1,
Egilsstaðir ∎ 471 2001 ∎ ⓀⓀ

Housed in the oldest building in town,
this restaurant has a lovely outdoor
patio. Its dinner menu focuses on
local ingredients including reindeer
and fish from the East Fjords. The
lunch menu offers well-priced
homecooked meals.

⑦ Aldan
MAP H3 ∎ Norðurgata 2,
710 Seyðisfjörður ∎ 472 1277 ∎ Ⓚ

This restaurant in Hótel Aldan *(see
p132)* is great for a three-course
meal. They also offer fish and chips.

⑧ Hótel Framtið
MAP G4 ∎ Vogaland 4, 765
Djúpivogur ∎ 478 8887 ∎ ⓀⓀ

Fill up on hearty fish dishes and roast
lamb fillet with thyme sauce at this
eatery in Hótel Framtið *(see p130)* on
Djúpivogur's harbour.

⑨ Álfacafé
MAP H2 ∎ Borgafjörður
Eystri ∎ 862 9802, 472 9900 ∎ Ⓚ

Housed inside a former fish factory
near Borgafjörður Eystri's old harbour,
Álfacafé serves light meals and sandwiches. It features heavy tables and
crockery made out of solid stone.

⑩ Pakkhús
MAP G5 ∎ Krosseyjarvegi 3, 780
Höfn í Hornafirði ∎ 478 2280 ∎ Closed
mid-Dec–mid-Jan ∎ www.pakkhus.is
∎ ⓀⓀⓀ

The wonderful Pakkhús *(see p62)* has
the perfect ambience for their special
langoustine by the harbour.

See map on p100 ←

TOP 10 South Iceland

South Iceland has a rich band of coastline, minor icecaps, fertile river plains and explosive volcanic landscapes, all wrapped up in history and folklore. The Blue Lagoon and the "Golden Circle", which includes Þingvellir, Geysir and Gullfoss, are Iceland's most iconic sights. There is also the Hekla volcano, a wealth of saga locations, waterfalls, hiking grounds, the gem-like Westman Islands and peaceful Vík village, all in easy reach of Reykjavík. You will need more time to reach Kirkjubæjarklaustur town, the Jökulsárlón glacial lagoon and the fringes of Vatnajökull National Park.

The Blue Lagoon

1 Þingvellir National Park

This amazing rift valley (*see pp12–13*), now a UNESCO World Heritage site, was the setting for Iceland's open-air parliament in Viking times. Stop at the Visitor Centre on the way along Route 36 for superlative views over the rift walls and the lava plains. Pick out key features such as the Law Rock, Þingvellir Church, Almannagjá canyon, Öxarárfoss waterfall, Þingvallavatn lake and the Skjaldbreiður volcano.

Öxará river, Þingvellir National Park

SOUTH ICELAND

0 kilometres 40

0 miles 40

Previous pages Kirkjugólf ("The Church Floor"), Kirkjubæjarklaustur

Gullfoss, Iceland's most dramatic waterfall

2 Gullfoss

The final stop on a tour of the "Golden Circle", Gullfoss *(see pp18–19)* is Iceland's most dramatic waterfall and it is deafening, except in winter. Make sure you get a look at it from as many viewpoints as possible – especially from the top of the canyon, where you can appreciate the Hvítá river's journey from the barren Interior to the north.

3 Geysir

It is incredible to find such a raw, primal sight as Geysir's scalding waterspouts erupting by the side of the main road. Just 90 minutes from the capital, Geysir has a hotel, petrol station and tourist centre. The key geyser to watch is Strokkur, which erupts every few minutes. Geysir itself, meanwhile, is no longer particularly active – you would be very lucky to see it erupt. The whole site *(see pp16–17)* is surrounded by a collection of smaller hot pools, each with its own distinct character.

4 The Blue Lagoon

Iceland's southwest extreme, the Reykjanes peninsula, is almost entirely covered in barren lava fields, which makes finding the vivid Blue Lagoon *(see pp14–15)* hidden within it doubly surprising. Making creative use of waste water from a geothermal power plant, the Blue Lagoon offers an outstanding experience of outdoor soaking. Its white silt is said to have health benefits, too.

5 Þjórsárdalur

MAP D5 ■ Both access roads subject to closure ■ Þjóðveldisbærinn: Open Jun–Aug: 10am–6pm daily; www.thjodveldisbaer.is ■ Þjórsárdalslaug: see www.swimminginiceland.com for latest information ■ Adm

Þjórsárdalur is a broad, stark river valley, which was shaped by an eruption in 1102 of the Hekla volcano *(see p46)*, just one ridge away to the east. The eruption buried a Viking longhouse up the valley at Stöng, which has now been excavated and is open to the public, reached via a gravel track, with a full reconstruction nearby at Þjóðveldisbærinn. There is a swimming pool in the small village of Árnes, next to the Þjórsárstofa visitor centre.

Hamarinn
△ 1,573 m

Grímsvötn
△ 1,719 m

Vatnajökull

Jökulsárlón **10**

Skaftafell ●

Lómagnúpur

Kirkjubæjarklaustur
9

Fagurhólsmýri

1 Top 10 Sights
see pp108–11

1 Places to Eat
see p113

1 The Best of the Rest
see p112

6 Fljótshlíð

MAP D5 ▪ Saga Centre: open Jun–mid-Sep: 9am–6pm daily; adm; www.sagatrail.is

To reach the Markarfljót river, take Route 1 to Hvolsvöllur township – where you should visit the excellent Saga Centre – and then follow the 30-km- (19-mile-) long Route 261 east. The area is central to key scenes from *Njál's Saga*, including the farm Völlur, where the tale opens, and Hlíðarendi, home to the virtuous Gunnar Hámundarson. There is a church on the hillside at Hlíðarendi today, from which you can look seawards over the valley, where landmarks like rocky Stóri-Dímon stand proud.

NJÁL'S SAGA

This saga is a gripping account of a bloody, 50-year-long family feud revolving around the household of Njáll Þorgeirsson, in which the evil scheming of Mörð Valgarðsson causes the deaths of both Njáll and his friend Gunnar Hámundarson. The hard-boiled delivery is softened by deadpan humour and vivid insights into daily life during Viking times.

7 Vestmannaeyjar

MAP C6 ▪ Daily ferry from Landeyjahöfn (from Þorlákshöfn in bad weather), flights from Reykjavík and Bakki

The Westman Islands are a string of volcanic outcrops off the south coast, which include one of the world's newest islands, Surtsey. Heimaey, the largest and only inhabited island in the group, is famous for the 1973 Eldfell eruption, which partially buried Heimaey town and almost ended its fishing industry. Visitors can climb Eldfell's still-steaming slopes or walk around the coast in half a day. The museum Eldheimar has exhibits on the Heimaey and Surtsey eruptions. Another highlight is the annual Þjóðhátíð festival (see p68) held here.

8 Vík

MAP D6

This peaceful seafront community of around 300 people is located below Reynisfjall's cliffs. Vík boasts a dramatic black-sand beach, great views east over the flat Mýrdalssandur black-lava desert, lively bird colonies and some towering offshore black stacks known as the Troll Rocks. Skógar and its waterfall, Skógafoss (see p45) are 30 minutes up the road and there are more seascapes to be

View from the top of Eldfell volcano, Vestmannaeyjar

enjoyed to the west at Reynisfjall and Dyrhólaey (see p50). Also close by are a number of walking tracks.

Kirkjubæjarklaustur
MAP E5

A tiny highway town in the middle of nowhere, Kirkjubæjarklaustur is surrounded by pseudocraters and hexagonal lava pavements known as Kirkjugólf ("The Church Floor"), with summer access to the Lakagígar craters (see p46). Moving east, Skaftafell in Vatnajökull National Park (see pp24–5) is an hour's drive away, on the other side of the black, sandy Skeiðarársandur desert. About 11 km (7 miles) south of Kirkjubæjarklaustur is Fjaðrárgljúfur, a canyon thought to be formed during the last Ice Age.

Icebergs at Jökulsárlón

Jökulsárlón
MAP G5

This is an essential stop on the long journey between Vík and Höfn. The icebergs, glacier tongue and rushing waters of Jökulsárlón – not to mention the bizarre sight of ice boulders on the beach – break the monotony of the bleak expanses of black gravel along the coastal fringes (see pp32–3). Seals are the pick of the wildlife commonly encountered here, although there is also plenty of birdlife to look out for. Lagoon cruises lasting about half an hour are an option during the summer months.

A DAY IN SOUTH ICELAND

▶ MORNING

Begin a classic "Golden Circle" tour by heading northeast from Reykjavík up Route 36, looking out along the way for the boxy, two-storey white house of the late author and Nobel Laureate Halldór Laxness. After passing Þingvallavatn's blue expanse you arrive on the west side of the Þingvellir rift valley (see pp12–13), where it is time to spend an hour – or the entire day – soaking up the history and landscapes at Iceland's cultural heart. Cross the rift and take Route 365 to Laugarvatn (see p59), where you could stop and have a swim at the National School for Sports, before pressing further along Routes 37 and 35 to spectacular water features at Geysir (see pp16–17) and Gullfoss (see pp18–19).

AFTERNOON

Have lunch at either Hótel Geysir (see p113), where you can get a three-course meal, or at Gullfoss' Visitor Centre, whose café does excellent lamb soup. Then follow Route 35 southwest to Skálholt (see p39), a bishopric and educational centre since the 11th century. Route 35 continues southwest from Skálholt past the Kerið crater (see p112) to Selfoss, a busy town on the Ölfusá river, where the bridge was the cause of Iceland's first strike. The highway runs straight back to Reykjavík via the greenhouses at Hveragerði (see p112), which are famous for their flowers and vegetables. Or you can detour coastwards to Stokkseyri and Eyrarbakki (see p112).

See map on pp108–9 ←

The Best of the Rest

1 Mýrdalsjökull
MAP D6 ■ www.mountain
guides.is ■ www.arcanum.is

This icecap conceals the infamous
Katla volcano (see p47). The lowest
glacier tongue, Sólheimajökull, is
accessible off Route 1. Here, you
can kayak, hike the glacier or ride
a snowmobile.

2 Kerið
MAP C5

This deep but small crater north of
Selfoss is best viewed on a sunny
day to appreciate the red and black
slopes contrasting with the water.

3 Seljavallalaug
MAP D6 ■ Seljavellir

Surrounded by scenic glaciers and
volcanoes, soak in the warm waters
of this open-air geothermal pool,
which is also the oldest swimming
pool in Iceland.

4 Inside the Volcano
MAP C5 ■ Open mid-May–Oct
■ Tour duration: 5–6 hours ■ Adm
■ www.insidethevolcano.com

Be lowered in an open-sided cage
120 m (390 ft) into the huge magma
chamber of a dormant volcano for
a fascinating experience.

The Inside the Volcano tour

5 Leirubakki
MAP D5 ■ Route 26 ■ 487 8700
■ Summer buses between Reykjavík
and Landmannalaugar ■ www.
leirubakki.is

Farm and hotel near Mount Hekla
(see p31), with a volcano museum
and a lava-block hot tub with views
of the mountain.

6 Bridge Between Continents
MAP C5

The European and American
continental plates separate visibly
at Þingvellir – cross between them
on this bridge, a 20-minute drive
from the Blue Lagoon or Keflavík.

7 Hveragerði
MAP C5

Hveragerði is Iceland's major
greenhouse town, using geothermal
heat to grow flowers and vegetables
on a commercial scale. There are
hiking trails and a swimming pool.

8 Hvolsvöllur Saga Centre
MAP C6 ■ Hlíðarvegur 14,
Hvolsvöllur ■ 487 8781 ■ Open
summer: 11:30am–11pm daily;
winter: 10am–5pm Sat & Sun ■ Adm
■ www.sagatrail.is

Lively exhibition dedicated to the
Viking era and the world of sagas.

9 Lava Centre
MAP C6 ■ Hvolsvöllur
■ 415 5200 ■ Open 9am–5pm daily
(restaurant open till 8pm) ■ Adm
■ www.lavacentre.is

This interactive high-tech exhibition
explores the country's geologic
activity, from volcano explosions and
earthquakes to glacial floods. There
is also a decent restaurant, a gift store
and an observation deck on site.

10 Stokkseyri and Eyrarbakki
MAP C5 ■ www.husid.com

Delightful villages with great seafood
restaurants and the Húsið museum.

Places to Eat

1 Hótel Rangá
MAP C5 ▪ Ringroad, near Hella ▪ 487 5700 ▪ ⓀⓀ

Nordic-European cuisine is served at this splendid hotel restaurant (see p131) with views of the finest salmon river in Iceland. Be sure to try their signature dish featuring salmon.

2 Krisp
MAP C5 ▪ Eyravegur 8, Selfoss ▪ 482 4099 ▪ Ⓚ

Local cuisine presented with an Asian twist. Great salads and steaks.

3 Hótel Geysir
MAP C5 ▪ Haukadalur, Geysir ▪ 480 6800 ▪ ⓀⓀ

Generous breakfast and lunch buffets, an à la carte dinner menu and great views of the Geysir area make this hotel-restaurant (see p17) the best place to eat in the area.

4 Hótel Selfoss
MAP C5 ▪ Eyravegur 2, Selfoss ▪ 480 2500 ▪ ⓀⓀ

This up-market option serves a well-presented menu of Icelandic seafood and meat staples.

5 Gullfoss Kaffi
MAP D4 ▪ Gullfoss ▪ 486 6500 ▪ Ⓚ

With wide vistas of the surrounding landscape – though not of Gullfoss itself – this spacious, wooden-framed café is a great spot to pull up for a bowl of lamb soup.

6 Hótel Flúðir
MAP C5 ▪ Vesturbrún 1, Flúðir ▪ 486 6630 ▪ ⓀⓀ

An Isolated modern building on the edge of a farming town, Hótel Flúðir has splendid views and a menu featuring locally grown greenhouse vegetables and meats.

7 Rauða Húsið
MAP C5 ▪ Búðarstíg 4, Eyrarbakki ▪ 483 3330 ▪ ⓀⓀ

A good reason to visit the charming Eyrarbakki village, this restaurant in a historic house offers splendid lobster, lamb and fish dishes at a fraction of their cost in Reykjavík.

Lobster dish at Rauða Húsið

8 Hafið Bláa
MAP C5 ▪ Þorlákshöfn, near Óseyrar Bridge, Eyrarbakki ▪ 483 1000 ▪ Ⓚ

With stunning surround views, this is another excellent dining experience at the mouth of the Ölfusá river. The menu is dominated by an exceptional selection of lobster and fish dishes.

9 Kaffi Duus
MAP B5 ▪ Duusgata 10, Keflavík ▪ 421 7080 ▪ ⓀⓀ

This smart place is not far from the Keflavík International Airport, which makes it an ideal location to tuck into tasty lamb, lobster and salmon dishes before heading homewards.

10 Fjöruborðið
MAP C5 ▪ Eyrarbraut 3a, 825 Stokkseyri ▪ 483 1550 ▪ www.fjorubordid.is ▪ ⓀⓀ

Located in the village of Stokkseyri, this restaurant (see p63) features an elaborate food and drinks menu with separate meal options for kids.

See map on pp108–9

🔟 The Highland Interior

Icelandic horse, Hekla

Inland from the relatively fertile coastline is Iceland's Highland Interior. This is a beautiful wilderness of black gravel, lava plains and glaciated peaks that have been blasted by summer storms and winter frosts. Not surprisingly, the Interior is uninhabited, but the ghosts of numerous pack-horse trails have now been graded for 4WDs only. Open for a few weeks in summer, the most accessible of these routes are the Kjölur (from Gullfoss to near Akureyri) and Fjallabak (from Hella to Kirkjubæjarklaustur). Long-distance buses follow these routes from June to September.

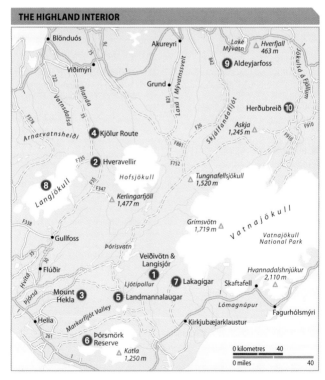

THE HIGHLAND INTERIOR

- Blönduós
- Akureyri
- Laké Mývatn
- Hverfjall 463 m
- ⑨ Aldeyjarfoss
- Víðimýri
- Grund
- Herðubreið ⑩
- Askja 1,245 m
- Arnarvatnsheiði
- ④ Kjölur Route
- ② Hveravellir
- Hofsjökull
- Tungnafellsjökull 1,520 m
- ⑧
- Langjökull
- Kerlingarfjöll 1,477 m
- Grímsvötn 1,719 m
- Vatnajökull
- Vatnajökull National Park
- Gullfoss
- Þórisvatn
- Veiðivötn & Langisjór ①
- Hvannadalshnjúkur 2,110 m
- Flúðir
- Ljótipollur
- ⑦ Lakagígar
- Skaftafell
- Mount Hekla ③
- ⑤ Landmannalaugar
- Lómagnúpur
- Fagurhólsmýri
- Hella
- Markarfljót Valley
- Kirkjubæjarklaustur
- ⑥ Þórsmörk Reserve
- Katla 1,250 m

0 kilometres 40
0 miles 40

Panoramic view of the spectacular Langisjór lake

1 Veiðivötn and Langisjór
MAP E5

Veiðivötn and Langisjór are part of a complex of inland waterways inside volcanic "stretch marks" southwest of Vatnajökull *(see p24)*, reached off the F208 Fjallabak Route. There are good fishing areas amidst the stark countryside. Veiðivötn is an area of tarns and streams, while Langisjór is a narrow stretch of water. Both are accessible only along rough tracks and there is no public transport.

2 Hveravellir
MAP D4 ■ Summer buses from Reykjavík and Akureyri ■ Bus schedules: www.sba.is

Halfway along the Kjölur Route, Hveravellir is a desolate hot springs area with an outdoor hot tub, calcified mounds bubbling boiling water, a strong smell of sulphur and a basic hut with bunk beds run by the Icelandic Touring Association.

3 Mount Hekla
East of Þjórsá river is Mount Hekla *(see p31)*, which means "hooded", after the clouds that obscure its summit. It was once believed to be the entrance to hell, due to its eruptions followed by months of noisy "grumbling" (taken to be the sound of tormented souls). On a good day, you can see the mountain from Hella on Route 1, and you will pass close to it en route to Landmannalaugar. Many companies run 4WD circuits and trips to the mountain in summer.

4 The Kjölur Route
MAP D4 ■ Bus schedule: www.bsi.is, www.sba.is ■ Road: open mid-Jun–late Aug

The Kjölur Route (Kjalvegur) is the easiest of the Highland roads to traverse, running for 170 km (106 miles) from Gullfoss *(see pp18–19)* to Route 1 near Blönduós *(see p95)*. All the major rivers have been bridged and the gravel track is safe for cars. Sights along the way include Hveravellir's hot springs and the Langjökull icecap.

5 Landmannalaugar
MAP D5 ■ Bus schedule: www.re.is

Relatively accessible and just 3 or 4 hours' drive from Reykjavík, Landmannalaugar delivers a full-on Highland experience. The road takes in volcanic wastelands, river crossings, mountains and hot springs. There are hills, lava fields and lakes to explore. You could even stay at the bunkhouse or the campsite and spend 4 days hiking to Þórsmörk along the Laugavegur trail *(see p55)*.

Laugavegur hiking trail

Þórsmörk Reserve
MAP D6 ▪ Bus schedule: www.
re.is, www.trex.is ▪ Accessible during
summer only

Iceland's most popular hiking area
(see p55), Þórsmörk is accessible
by 4WD from the highway near
Hvolsvöllur via the 30-km- (19-mile-)
long F249 – watch out for the potentially dangerous river crossing at
the end. It is also accessible by
trekking along Laugavegur or
from Skógar via Fimmvörðuháls
(see p54). Set in an exceptionally
pretty glacial valley, the pick of
the views at Þórsmörk are from
Valahnúkur (an easy and short
ascent) and Útigönguhöfði (an
arduous and long ascent).

Lakagígar
MAP E5

This 25-km- (16-mile-) long row
of craters erupted with a vengeance
in 1783 (see p25), disrupting weather
patterns all across Europe and
nearly depopulating Iceland. Walking
trails ranging in length between
20 minutes and 2 hours allow you
to explore the line of cones and
expansive lava fields, which are now
partly buried under a thick matting
of moss and heather. There is
no accommodation on site, but
mountain huts and campsites can
be found along the road. Seasonal

HIGHLAND DRIVING

Rough conditions, no settlements
and nobody to help if something
goes wrong all make it imperative
that Highland roads are tackled only
in an approved rental car. Travel in
convoy, check road conditions before
setting out (www.safetravel.is) and give
your route and estimated arrival time
to someone reliable so rescue can be
organized if needed.

buses from Skaftafell run here via
Kirkjubæjarklaustur and the 60-km-
(37-mile-) long F206.

 Langjökull
MAP D4 ▪ Year-round
Jeep tours from Reykjavík
▪ www.adventures.is

Iceland's second largest icecap,
the "Long Glacier" west of the
Kjölur Route feeds Hvítárvatn and
Sandvatn lakes, which in turn drain
into the Hvítá river, on which the
spectacular Gullfoss waterfalls are
located (see pp18–19). There is talk
of damming another of Langjökull's
lakes, Hagavatn, for hydropower,
although there is opposition to this
plan. Apart from seeing the glacier
from the Kjölur or Kaldidalur routes,
tours run up here for snowmobiling
trips – you only get an hour but it
is an exhilarating experience.

Langjökull, Iceland's second largest icecap

⑨ Aldeyjarfoss
MAP E3 ■ Bus schedule: www.re.is

The surrounding rock formations are what make this waterfall, which sits on the Skjálfandafljót river, so striking. A layer of outlandishly fashioned basalt columns is capped by a thick blanket of solidified lava. Buses negotiating the Sprengisandur crossing between Reykjavík and Akureyri make it a point to stop here. To reach Aldeyjarfoss by car, take road 842 from Goðafoss (see p45) and then the mountain road F26. Although bumpy, the last few kilometers of gravel road are still suitable for cars without 4WD. Alternatively, it's possible to park at the intersection to road F26 and take a 45-minute hike to the waterfall.

Basalt columns at Aldeyjarfoss

⑩ Herðubreið
MAP F3

Known as the "Queen of the Icelandic Mountains", Herðubreið sits amid the mountain range east of Askja (see p21). Soaring to a height of 1,682 m (5,518 ft), it overlooks the Ódáðahraun ("Desert of Evil Deeds"). The slopes are laced with freshwater springs and covered with the Arctic river beauty flower in July. You get views of the mountain on a clear day from the road to Kárahnjúkar in Eyjabakkar (see p104). The surrounding area, Herdubreidarlindir, is worth exploring, and has a campground as well as hiking trails.

A DAY IN THE HIGHLANDS

▶ MORNING

Start early for this day trip to **Landmannalaugar** (see p115) and bring a packed lunch. The journey will take upwards of 8 hours, depending on how many times you stop along the way. Head east along Route 1 from Reykjavík via Selfoss and Hella, then turn north up Route 264 to see the Viking buildings at Keldur Farm. With **Mount Hekla** (see p115) looming behind, take a moment to appreciate Keldur's location – so close to an active volcano. Retrace the route towards Hella, then turn north along Route 268 for a half-hour run through lava fields to Mount Hekla and the intersection with Route 26. You could turn left here to **Leirubakki** (see p112), but for Landmannalaugar turn right, driving across the yellow pumice plain between Hekla and the Þjórsá river, before reaching the junction with F225, which heads east to Landmannalaugar. Pull up and enjoy your picnic lunch.

AFTERNOON

The F225 road traverses the black-sand wasteland of Hekla's northern foothills, with several river crossings before it reaches an intersection after 47 km (29 miles). Turn right (south) at this junction, which leads down to **Frostastaðavatn**'s (see p31) lakeshore and then right again onto the 5-km- (3-mile-) long F224, which crosses a double fjord before reaching Landmannalaugar. Here, take in the unique landscapes while hiking around the area, and finish by soaking in the geothermal river surrounded by colourful rhyolite mountains.

See map on p114 ←

Streetsmart

Mount Esja dominating the
Reykjavík skyline

Getting Around	120
Practical Information	122
Places to Stay	128
General Index	134
Acknowledgments	140
Phrase Book	142
Map Index	144

Getting Around

Arriving by Air

Most flights from Europe, the USA and Canada land at **Keflavík International Airport**, 50 km (31 miles) from Reykjavík. The national carrier of Iceland is **Icelandair**. **PLAY Airlines** is another option. It takes about 3 hours to reach Iceland from Europe and 5–6 hours from the USA.

The cheapest way into town from Keflavík is the **Flybus**, which delivers arrivals to the **BSÍ** long-distance bus station and major hotels in Reykjavík in about 45 mins. Taxis have fixed rates but are expensive. You can arrange to collect rental cars at the airport.

Some flights from Greenland and the Faroe Islands use **Reykjavík International Airport**, just west of the city centre.

Reykjavík International Airport also offers direct domestic flights with **Eagle Air** to Akureyri, Egilsstaðir, Húsavík, the Westman Islands, Ísafjörður, Höfn, Sauðárkrókur, Gjögur and Bíldudalur. From Akureyri, there are connections to Grímsey, Vopnafjörður and Thorshöfn. Regional airports generally stay open in winter, when roads might be closed.

Arriving by Sea

From April until the end of October, the **Smyril Line** runs a weekly passenger and vehicle ferry between Denmark and Seyðisfjörður in eastern Iceland. It costs more than flying, and the 3-day crossing can be rough, but you visit the Faroe Islands en route and it's the only way to bring your own vehicle into Iceland. International cruise boats also visit Iceland in the summer, docking at Reykjavík, Akureyri, Ísafjörður and Seyðisfjörður.

Bus Travel

The main public transport operator in Iceland is **Strætó**, who runs buses in both Reykjavík and around the country. In the city centre, the buses are yellow in colour, while those outside of Reykjavík are blue-and-yellow or white.

The flat fare for a single ticket is ISK550; a discount is available for children, people with disabilities and the elderly. You can buy a single ticket on board the bus using cash and, outside of the capital, card. Drivers cannot give change if you pay with cash. Packs of 20 single tickets and bus cards allowing travel for 1–12 months can be bought via the Strætó website, at Reykjavík's Mjóddin bus station or at other vendors around the city. There's also the Strætó app, which allows users to plan journeys, buy tickets and track bus locations in real time.

Strætó's website has information on safety and hygiene measures, tickets, timetables, transport maps and more.

There are a number of private bus companies that operate in Iceland. From the BSÍ station, **Reykjavík Excursions** runs day tours throughout Iceland. During the summer it runs the Highland Bus services in cooperation with **SBA-Norðurleið**, who offer tours in the north of Iceland. Similar operators include **Grayline** and **TREX** in Reykjavík. Other parts of the country are covered by local operators. While most destinations are served daily in summer, all Interior services, even those along the Ringroad between Höfn and Egilsstaðir, stop or are reduced at other times.

Passes that restrict you to a specific route and schedule are cheaper than paying for separate journeys. Book bus seats at least a day in advance.

Driving

You can bring your car to Iceland on the Smyril Line ferry from Denmark. There are car-rental agencies, such as **Iceland Car Rental**, though rates are high. The minimum age for renting a car is 20 (25 for Jeeps). Rental cars might not be insured for some routes. All European and US driving licences are valid in Iceland. UK visitors need to bring both parts of their licence.

Seatbelts are compulsory and headlights must always be on. Driving is on the right-hand side. Speed limits are 90 kmph (56 mph) on asphalt roads, 80 kmph (50 mph) on gravel roads and 30 kmph (19 mph) in residential areas. Drink-driving and driving off marked roads or tracks are illegal.

Route 1, or the Ringroad, runs a circuit 1,300 km (808 miles) around Iceland. Many country roads are unsealed gravel and not suited to fast driving. Roads marked on a map with an F require 4WD at all times. Fill up your fuel tank when you can as smaller towns might not have pumps and they can be far apart.

Bad weather can make any road dangerous for conventional vehicles. Many 4WD routes cross dangerous rivers, snowfields and sands, and are suitable for experienced drivers only. Some car-rental agencies offer GPS rental. **Road Conditions** provides daily updates about the road conditions and the weather.

Taxis

Taxis in Iceland are metered and have uniform fares. There is no tipping. Look for ranks outside major hotels or call for one. **Taxi Reykjavík** offers 24-hour service.

Ferries

Ferries run to a number of offshore islands. Daily services operated by Eimskip go to the Westman Islands from Landeyjahöfn in the south (about 30 mins). Samskip ferries run to Grímsey and Hrísey in the north, and Stykkishólmur–Flatey–Brjánslækur in the west.

Cycling

Cycling is an inexpensive way of seeing the country in summer, though come prepared for unsealed gravel roads and unkind weather. You need to be fit, experienced in repairing your bike, and to carry spares. You also need a tent and cooking gear and supplies, as there can be considerable distances between towns. There are several bike-hire shops in Reykjavík and Akureyri, but little assistance elsewhere. It is only permitted to cycle on roads or marked tracks.

Walking

Iceland's cities and towns are easily walkable, thanks to their relatively small size and prevalence of dedicated pathways. The country also has many hiking trails. Accommodation is either camping or using hiking-organization huts. Both need to be prebooked. Come equipped for bad weather and rough terrain (including river crossings). Carry all necessary gear, such as food, water and maps or a GPS. Some routes may also require crampons and an ice axe. Iceland's two hiking organizations, **Útivist** and **Ferðafélag Íslands**, can offer advice.

DIRECTORY

ARRIVING BY AIR

BSÍ
[580 5400
w bsi.is

Eagle Air
w eagleair.is

Flybus
[580 5400
w re.is/flybus

Icelandair
w icelandair.com

Keflavík International Airport
w kefairport.is

PLAY Airlines
w flyplay.com

Reykjavík International Airport
w isavia.is

ARRIVING BY SEA

Smyril Line
[298 354 900
w smyrilline.com

BUS TRAVEL

Gray Line
[540 1313
w grayline.is

Reykjavík Excursions
[580 5400
w re.is

SBA-Norðurleið
[550 0700
w sba.is

Strætó
[540 2700
w straeto.is

TREX
[587 6000
w trex.is

DRIVING

Iceland Car Rental
[415 2500
w icelandcarrental.is

Road Conditions
w road.is

TAXIS

Taxi Reykjavík
[561 0000

FERRIES

Samskip
[458 8000
w landflutningar.is/saefari

Eimskip
[433 2254
w seatours.is

WALKING

Ferðafélag Íslands
w fi.is/en

Útivist
w utivist.is/english

Practical Information

Passports and Visas

For entry requirements, including visas, consult your nearest Icelandic embassy or check the **Directorate of Immigration**'s website.

From late 2023, citizens of the UK, US, Canada, Australia and New Zealand do not need a visa for stays of up to three months, but must apply in advance for the European Travel Information and Authorization System (**ETIAS**). Visitors from other countries may also require an ETIAS, so check before travelling. EU nationals do not need a visa or an ETIAS.

Government Advice

Now more than ever, it is important to consult both your and the Icelandic government's advice before travelling. The **UK Foreign, Commonwealth & Development Office (FCDO)**, the **US State Department**, the **Australian Department of Foreign Affairs and Trade** and the Icelandic **Safe Travel** website offer the latest information on security, health and local regulations.

Customs Information

You can find information on the laws relating to goods and currency taken in or out of Iceland on **Iceland Revenue and Customs** website.

Passengers over 18 may import 200 cigarettes or 250 g (8.8 oz) of tobacco products. Those over 20 may also bring a litre of spirits, a litre of wine and 6 litres of beer. Visitors can import 3 kg (7 lb) of food duty-free, but no meat unless canned or boiled. Riding clothing and angling gear must be disinfected and certified by a vet before entry. Used riding gear cannot be bought. It is illegal to take whale products from Iceland into the UK or EU.

Vehicles, with up to 200 litres (44 gal) of fuel in built-in fuel tanks, can be brought in tax-free on the Smyril Line ferry to Seyðisfjörður, providing that you stay less than a year in Iceland, use the vehicle for personal travel only and take it with you on leaving. European drivers who bring their own vehicles do not need a Green Card or proof of third-party insurance; but, international automobile insurance may be required.

Insurance

We recommend that you take out a comprehensive insurance policy covering theft, loss of belongings, medical care, cancellations and delays. Remember to read the small print carefully, including any policy exclusions – especially if you're planning on hiking or adventure travel.

UK citizens are eligible for free emergency medical care in Iceland provided they have a valid European Health Insurance Card (EHIC). Note that the UK Global Health Insurance Card (GHIC) does not cover travellers to Iceland. Private medical insurance is therefore recommended.

Health

Iceland has a world-class healthcare system. Emergency medical care in Iceland is free for all UK citizens, who have an EHIC; be sure to present this card as soon as possible. You may have to pay after treatment and reclaim the money later.

For other visitors, including UK citizens without EHICs, payment of medical expenses is the patient's responsibility. It is therefore important to arrange comprehensive medical insurance before you travel.

No vaccinations are required for Iceland. Tap water is safe to drink everywhere. You are advised to bring all medications you might need with you.

Iceland's major hospitals include **Akureyri Hospital** and **Landspítali University Hospital.** Ambulances incur a nonrefundable cost. Pharmacies (apótek) are in almost every town and often stay open late.

Smoking, Alcohol and Drugs

Smoking is prohibited in bars, restaurants, clubs and cafés. There are no designated smoking areas inside and smoking outside is restricted to certain areas. It is forbidden to smoke on public transport.

The legal drinking age in Iceland is 20 years. It is

prohibited to drive under the influence of alcohol or other substances; those caught doing so will be fined and may temporarily or permanently lose their driving licence.

Alcohol is sold through state-controlled shops (Vínbúðin) and is highly taxed; because of the cost of alcohol, it is considered normal not to buy rounds, and even to sip on one drink for the entire evening, though many bars have happy hours.

Penalties for possession, use and trafficking of drugs are severe; large fines and custodial sentences can be imposed.

ID

You will need photo ID when buying alcohol, and often for entry into bars. It is not a legal requirement to carry picture ID at all times in Iceland but a valid driving licence will be required if you want to rent a car.

Personal Security

Iceland is a safe country, with a low crime rate, but it is always best to take the usual safety precautions. Always lock your car, don't leave valuables on display and don't flash your cash. Keep an extra eye on your belongings when you are in crowds, on public transport or queuing at busy tourist attractions. Minor assaults, petty burglary and drug-related crimes do occur, primarily in Reykjavík.

If you have anything stolen, report the crime within 24 hours to the nearest police station and take ID with you. Get a copy of the crime report to

make an insurance claim. All of the **Emergency Services** (police, fire service and ambulance) can be contacted by dialling 112.

As a rule, Icelanders are very accepting of all people, regardless of their race, gender or sexuality. Homosexuality was legalized in 1940 and in 2010, Iceland became the ninth country in the world to recognize same-sex marriage. The Reykjavík Pride festival, held in August, is one of the country's most popular festivals. **Gaylceland** has useful information on the LGBTQ+ scene in Reykjavík, and **Gayice** offers advice for LGBTQ+ travellers visiting Iceland.

Sexual harassment is not a common problem in Iceland. However, if you ever feel threatened, head straight to the nearest police station.

When visiting Iceland, remember to bring warm, wind- and water-proof clothes as the weather can be unpredictable. You'll also need sunglasses, sunscreen and a hat, especially if you are planning to hike. Hikers also need tough boots for lava, snow and rain.

Be aware of natural hazards: you'll find very few warning signs or safety barriers even at heavily touristed sights such as waterfalls, geysers or boiling mud pits. Unbridged river crossings are dangerous, whether on foot or in a vehicle. Hiking trails are often poorly marked; hikers should be able to navi-gate in poor conditions. Avalanches

have claimed many lives in Iceland over the years; you should always check warnings before hiking, especially in the West and East Fjords. If swimming, be aware that the coastline and beaches are typically not guarded.

DIRECTORY

PASSPORTS AND VISAS
Directorate of Immigration
w utl.is

ETIAS
w etiasvisa.com

GOVERNMENT ADVICE
Australian Department of Foreign Affairs and Trade
w smartraveller.gov.au

UK Foreign, Commonwealth & Development Office (FCDO)
w gov.uk/foreign-traveladvice

US Department of State
w state.gov/travel

Safe Travel
w safetravel.is

CUSTOMS INFORMATION
Iceland Revenue and Customs
w customs.is

HEALTH
Akureyri Hospital
Eyrarlandsvegur
C 463 0100

Landspítali University Hospital
■ Hringbraut 101, Reykjavík
C 543 1000

PERSONAL SECURITY
Emergency Services
C 112

Gayice
w gayice.is

Gaylceland
w gayiceland.is

Travellers with Specific Requirements

The cities of Reykjavík and Akureyri both have relatively good facilities for travellers with specific requirements. The capital is particularly accommodating: all of its buses are wheelchair accessible and many of its hotels, restaurants and businesses are either accessible or able to provide the relevant services if notified in advance. Some museums, such as the Settlement Exhibition (see p75) and the Reykjavík Maritime Musem (see p41), also have good wheelchair access.

Outside of these cities accessibility can be lacking, especially in more remote areas. However, some sights, including the Blue Lagoon (see p14), have good accessibility, and several tour companies, such as **Nordic Visitor** and **Iceland Unlimited**, offer specialist holiday packages.

Other useful information sources include: **Thekkingarmidstod Sjalfsbjargar**, which has advice on travelling with a physical disability in Iceland; **Wheelmap**, which provides information on wheelchair accessibility; and the TravAble app, which offers detailed information about accessible sights in Reykjavík. While it does not directly cater to tourists, **Sjálfsbjörg Association for Disabled People** may provide advice.

Time Zone

Iceland follows Greenwich Mean Time (GMT) and is 5 hours ahead of US Eastern Standard Time. It does not observe Daylight Saving Time.

Money

Iceland's currency is the króna (ISK) or krónur in the plural. Foreign currency is accepted at Keflavík International Airport and in a few shops in Reykjavík.

Contactless payments are now widely accepted across Iceland, and on many buses it is now common to pay using an app.

Banks are found in all major towns, many with 24-hour ATMs outside issuing krónur. You'll also find ATMs in larger stores, malls and at petrol stations. MasterCard and Visa are widely accepted by ATMs and businesses across the country but many places won't handle American Express.

Although tipping is not common or expected it is always appreciated.

Electrical Appliances

Iceland has standard European electrical voltage and frequency (240 V, 50 Hz) so North American electrical devices will need converters. Plugs are European-style two-pin; UK and North American electrical appliances will need a special adapter.

Mobile Phones and Wi-Fi

Iceland's country code is 354; phone numbers within Iceland are seven digits long and have no area codes.

The mobile phone network is usuallly reliable in most parts of Iceland, although it can be patchy or non-existant in more remote areas. It is a GSM system, compatible with European networks but not US ones. Buy a prepaid local SIM card if yours doesn't work here. Central Iceland has Nordic Mobile Telephone (NMT) coverage, but you should only need this if you're travelling independently in the Interior. Contact vehicle-rental companies or hiking organizations about renting an NMT set.

Free Wi-Fi is available in many cafés and in some accommodation.

Postal Services

Post offices are in most major towns and are open 9am–4:30pm Monday–Friday, sometimes closing later in larger towns. Check website for further details on **Reykjavík central post office**. Stamps are also sold in hotels, bookshops and supermarkets.

Weather

Iceland's summer sun barely dips below the horizon at midnight. In winter you are lucky to get 4 hours of daylight, making November to February a great time to watch the aurora borealis. The climate is milder than you might expect. In the south of the country, winters average a bearable 0°C (32°F), while summer temperatures can reach 23°C (74°F), though rains can be frequent from spring to autumn. The north is generally colder, with heavy snowfalls in winter and temperatures dropping below -15°C (5°F), though the northeast is famously sunny in summer. The centre of the country is dominated by Vatnajökull, Europe's largest icecap, and the Highland Interior is uninhabited and usually snowbound for much of the year. Roads only open for a few weeks from mid-July until September.

Opening Hours

Shops open 10am–6pm Monday–Friday, and Saturday from 10am until between 1pm and 4pm. Some supermarkets are open daily until 11pm. Banks are open 9:15am–4pm Monday–Friday. Outside Reykjavík, the hours may be shorter. Museums have their own opening hours, and outside the capital they might be closed in winter.

Businesses, banks and most shops tend to be closed on public holidays.

The COVID-19 pandemic proved that situations can change suddenly. Always check before visiting attractions and hospitality venues for up-to-date hours and booking requirements.

Visitor Information

Visit Iceland, the country's official tourism website, has comprehensive information for visitors to the country; in addition, there are also separate websites for the different regions of the country – north, south, east and west – which can be accessed via the Visit Iceland website. Other good sources of general tourist information include the websites of the **Randburg Travellers' Guide**, **Visit Reykjavík** and **Safe Travel** *(see p122)*. For hikers and anglers, **Nordic Adventure Travel** is also useful.

Forlagið and Ferðakort publish road atlases and specialist maps that cover the country in detail and are useful for independent touring and hiking. You can buy a good range at bookshops in Reykjavík and Akureyri, plus a restricted selection at some tourist offices, supermarkets and roadhouses. Hiking organizations and the Icelandic National Parks office publish local maps, which are usually only available on site.

The Reykjavik City Card (purchased via the Visit Reykjavik website) offers free entry to a number of museums and galleries, discounts on various tours, shops and services, as well as free bus travel within the capital. Cards are available for 24, 48 or 72 hours. The **Iceland Coupons** app offers discounts across the country.

Sustainable Travel

Iceland runs almost completely on renewable energy, and sustainability is important to the tourism industry here. Visit Iceland has created an "Icelandic Pledge", which visitors can sign on their website before arriving. It encourages travellers to: follow leave-no-trace principles; stick to authorized trails and roads; use official campsites instead of wild camping; and reduce plastic waste by using reusable water bottles. The website also has an "Iceland Academy" which gives useful tips on how to travel safely and responsibly in Iceland.

DIRECTORY

TRAVELLERS WITH SPECIFIC REQUIREMENTS

Nordic Visitor
ⓦ nordicvisitor.com

Iceland Unlimited
ⓦ icelandunlimited.is

Sjálfsbjörg Association for Disabled People
ⓦ sjalfsbjorg.is

Thekkingarmidstod Sjalfsbjargar
ⓦ thekkingarmidstod.is/adgengi/accessible-tourism-in-iceland/

Wheelmap
ⓦ wheelmap.org

POSTAL SERVICES

Reykjavík central post office
MAP J4 ◼ Radisson BLU Hótel Saga, Hagatorgi, 107 Reykjavík
ⓦ postur.is

VISITOR INFORMATION

Iceland Coupons
ⓦ coupons.is

Nordic Adventure Travel
ⓦ nat.is

Promote Iceland
ⓦ iceland.is

Randburg Travellers' Guide
ⓦ randburg.is

Visit Iceland
ⓦ visiticeland.com

Visit Reykjavík
ⓦ visitreykjavik.is

Language

Icelandic is a difficult, complex language, with grammar similar in some ways to German or Latin; few foreigners even attempt to learn it. English is taught in Iceland from an early age and most people speak it well, although Icelanders will be happy to hear you speak in your mother tongue.

Local Customs

If you make eye contact on the street, expect an Icelander to say "Góðan daginn", which means "good day". When visiting an Icelander's home it is important to always leave your shoes at the door – keeping them on is considered extremely rude.

Taxes and Refunds

The standard VAT rate in Iceland is 24 per cent and the reduced rate is 11 per cent. Visitors to Iceland are eligible for VAT refunds for individual purchases over ISK 6,000. Refunds can be claimed upon departure. More information can be found on the website for the Iceland Revenue and Customs (see p122).

Trips and Tours

There are countless trips and tours on offer in Iceland, which allow you to enjoy the country's most exciting sights and experiences.

The **Golden Circle** tour run by Reykjavík Excursions (see p120) is a classic combination of history and landscape,

all within a stone's throw of Reykjavík. It takes in the Geysir hot springs, Gullfoss waterfalls and Þingvellir National Park. Reykjavík Excursions also run tours to **Lakagígar**, one of the world's largest lava fields and site of the terrible 1783 eruption.

Askja, a landscape of steaming volcanic craters in the northeast Interior, is where astronauts once trained for their moon landings and makes for an interesting day trip from Lake Mývatn.

For mountain trekking, try an introductory morning of ice climbing or tackle a hardcore ascent of Hvannadalshnúkur (Iceland's highest peak) with the specialist tour company **Icelandic Mountain Guides**.

Go on a half-day **whale-watching** cruise from Húsavík in the northeast, or catch a boat out to either Lundey or Akurey near Reykjavík to go **puffin watching**.

Explore Iceland's remote interior on a **horseriding** trip. The country's unique, stocky horses arrived with the Vikings; in addition to walk, trot, gallop and canter, they have a "fifth gear", the *tölt*. Stables like Íshestar and Eldhestar offer everything from hour-long to multi-week expeditions.

Swimming

Bring your swimming gear as every town has an inexpensive *sundlaug* (public pool), geothermally heated to a constant temperature

of 28°C (83°F) and often with attached hot tubs and saunas. There is a strict pool etiquette to be followed: make sure you take your shoes off before entering the changing rooms, and shower without your costume before entering the pool area.

Out in the wilds, there are also many natural geothermal springs in places such as Mývatn, Landmannalaugar, and the artificial Blue Lagoon, which offer a fantastically atmospheric experience, especially during the winter months.

Dining

There is some excellent local food, worth perhaps splashing out for once in a smart restaurant. Seafood is top of the list, with superb Atlantic salmon, cod, trout, and char, not to mention lobster. Icelandic lamb is also very good. Other traditional foods include *harðfiðfiðfiskur* (wind-dried cod), a popular snack sometimes eaten with butter; *hangikjöt* (smoked lamb); *rjúpa* (ptarmigan), a grouse-like game bird; *súrmatur* (meats pickled in whey); and *hákarl* (fermented shark), an eye-wateringly pungent Icelandic speciality. Puffin is also considered a culinary tradition in Iceland. However, puffin numbers are declining (due to human activity and climate change) and limits to hunting seasons have now been put in place. For more information on Iceland's food scene, check out the **Iceland Local Food Guide**.

In terms of self-catering, Bónus, Krónan, Samkaup and Hagkaup are the most widespread supermarkets, with Bónus charging the lowest prices. Most villages will have somewhere to stock up, but the range might be limited and opening hours are often short in the countryside. In summer, fresh vegetables are easily available, especially in hothouse towns, where they are grown using geothermal methods. Many villages have bakeries, but rarely butchers or fishmongers.

Accommodation

Iceland's popularity has put a pressure on summer accommodation. It is advised to book beds in advance – even for hostels. Online booking is the norm everywhere.

You should always camp at a campsite, rather than wild camping. Check the **Envrionment Agency of Iceland** for more details on camping and campsites. Most people opt to use the well-equipped and inexpensive campsites found in even the smallest village. Most have toilets and showers. If there are no showers, head to the nearest public swimming pool. Make sure you have a weatherproof tent, a groundsheet, guy ropes and a variety of pegs, as rough ground and gale-force winds are a fact of life in Iceland. The very useful discount **Camping Card** will help campers save money across multiple campsites throughout the country.

In popular hiking areas, you will also find mountain huts run by the hiking organizations. These are usually chalet-style buildings, with dormitories, kitchens, toilets, showers and bunks or mattresses. Beds must be booked in advance and sleeping bags brought with you.

There are around 30 official hostels run by **HI Iceland** (a member of the Hostelling International network), ranging from a turf-roofed hut to multi-storey affairs with TVs, kitchens, cafés and tour desks. Hostel members get a discount on the room rate. Dormitories are the norm, but some have private rooms. Bring a sleeping bag or hire bedsheets if available.

Part-way between hostels and hotels, urban guesthouses and rural farmstays offer a broad range of self-catering facilities, sometimes in a main building, sometimes in separate chalets. For more information on farm holidays, visit **Hey Iceland**. Doubles or family rooms with made-up beds are usual, though some places offer a cheaper-rate option of sleeping bag accommodation, where you supply your own bedding. For an extra charge, meals can be prepared in advance.

There's a great variety of hotels within Iceland, ranging from simple to luxurious, with some offering stunning views of Iceland's spectacular landscapes. International airlines can sometimes offer attractive flight-and-accommodation packages and you'll find that prices drop considerably outside the main summer tourist season. An alternative is to use one of the summer-only **Hotel Eddas** scattered around the country, which serve as schools for the rest of the year. Rates are lower than ordinary hotels, rooms are functional and facilities are not too bad, often with restaurants or cafés, swimming pools and even local tours available.

DIRECTORY

TRIPS AND TOURS

Askja
w myvatntours.is

Golden Circle
w re.is

Icelandic Mountain Guides
w mountainguides.is

Lakagígar
w re.is

Puffin Watching
w elding.is

Whale Watching
w northsailing.is
w gentlegiants.is

Horseriding
w eldhestar.is
w ishestar.is

DINING

Iceland Local Food Guide
w icelandlocalfood.com

ACCOMMODATION

The Environment Agency of Iceland
w ust.is/english

Camping Card
w campingcard.is

Hey Iceland
w heyiceland.is

HI Iceland
w hostel.is

Hotel Eddas
w icelandairhotels.com

Places to Stay

PRICE CATEGORIES

For a standard double room per night (with breakfast if included), including taxes and extra charges.

Ⓚ under ISK20,000
ⓀⓀ ISK20,000–40,000
ⓀⓀⓀ over ISK40,000

Hotels in the Centre of Reykjavík

Canopy

MAP L2 ▪ Smiðjustígur 4 ▪ 528 7000 ▪ www.cano pyreykjavik.com ▪ ⓀⓀ
With a central location, stylish rooms and chic amenities, this four-star hotel is a swish and highly comfortable all-rounder. There's a good restaurant, a terrace space upstairs with a summer patio, and a 24-hour fitness area. You can even rent a record player and vinyl from the reception.

Center Hotels Klöpp

MAP M2 ▪ Klapparstígur 26 ▪ 595 8520 ▪ www. centerhotels.com ▪ ⓀⓀ
This is a streamlined place with comfortable rooms and open-plan bathrooms. Friendly, efficient and located just off bustling Laugarvegur, it is a sound option for a short stay. Rooms on the upper floors are quieter and some have sea views.

Fosshotel Lind

MAP N3 ▪ Rauðarárstígur 18 ▪ 562 3350 ▪ www. islandshotel.is ▪ ⓀⓀ
A reliable, comfortable hotel with good facilities and helpful staff. There is nothing lacking in the services offered, but the rooms are on the small and simple side. However, it is good for a brief stay.

Hótel Óðinsvé

MAP L3 ▪ Þórsgata 1 ▪ 511 6200 ▪ www. odinsve.is ▪ ⓀⓀ
Excellent value hotel that manages to balance the homey 1930s building with modern minimalist chic. Its location off the main streets means less likelihood of being disturbed by rowdy weekend merrymakers. The bistro-style SNAPS restaurant specializes in grills.

101 Hotel Reykjavík

MAP L2 ▪ Hverfisgata 10 ▪ 580 0101 ▪ www.101 hotel.is ▪ ⓀⓀⓀ
Close to the capital's main shopping street, this smart hotel is stark on the outside. Inside, the modern, bright rooms have a contemporary minimalist look, complete with wooden flooring, large beds and marble bathrooms. Amenities include a gym and spa.

Center Hotels Plaza

MAP K2 ▪ Aðalstræti 4–6 ▪ 595 8550 ▪ www. centerhotels.com ▪ ⓀⓀⓀ
Light, airy, modern building with rooms to match – timber flooring, white walls and furnishings. The suites have views of the older part of the city and there is an excellent choice of good restaurants nearby.

Hótel Borg

MAP L2 ▪ Pósthússtræti 11 ▪ 551 1440 ▪ www. hotelborg.is ▪ ⓀⓀⓀ
Art Deco building where old time elegance and modern style is reflected in the immaculate rooms, which are a showcase in sophistication, and come complete with genuine period furnishings. The hotel also has a spa and fitness room.

Hótel Holt

MAP L3 ▪ Bergstaðastræti 37 ▪ 552 5700 ▪ www. holt.is ▪ ⓀⓀⓀ
Holt's nondescript façade is deceptive – once through the doors you are in one of the most plush old-style hotels in town. It has the country's largest privately owned collection of 19th-century Icelandic artworks and an out-standing restaurant.

Hótel Reykjavík Centrum

MAP K2 ▪ Aðalstræti 16 ▪ 514 6000 ▪ www. islandshotel.is ▪ ⓀⓀⓀ
A modern hotel in an old building: the timber and red-corrugated-iron exterior sits above the remains of a 7th-century Viking settlement. The rooms have been tastefully modernized and there is a renowned res-taurant on the premises.

Hotels Around Reykjavík

Hótel Cabin

MAP N3 ▪ Borgartún 32, 105 Reykjavík ▪ 511 6030 ▪ www.hotelcabin.is ▪ Ⓚ
Tidy budget hotel with basic but clean furnishings

and three room categories, spanning compact rooms to superiors with a view. Some rooms are designed with inward-facing windows for relief during the bright summer nights. Great-value lunch buffet at the restaurant.

Hótel Laxnes
MAP Q5 ▪ Háholt 7, 270 Mosfellsbær ▪ 566 8822 ▪ www.hotellaxnes.is ▪ Ⓚ
A hotel in a semi-rural location, about a 20-minute bus ride from Reykjavík. The double rooms and apartments with kitchenettes are especially good and there's an outdoor hot tub with mountain views. There is a golf course and swimming pool nearby, and regular public buses into town.

Reykjavík City Hostel
MAP R3 ▪ Sundlaugarvegur 34, 105 Reykjavík ▪ 553 8110 ▪ www.hostel.is ▪ Ⓚ
One of the few Icelandic HI Hostels with private rooms as well as dormitories, which, along with its location near the Botanic Gardens and Laugardalur swimming pool, makes it the best budget option in town. Booking in advance is recommended.

Viking Village
MAP P6 ▪ Strandgata 55, 220 Hafnarfjörður ▪ 565 1213 ▪ www.fjorukrain.is ▪ Ⓚ
A whole complex built around a Viking theme, with accommodation, restaurants and Viking entertainment. The exterior of the hotel has a slight warehouse feel, but the rooms are

surprisingly good. There are also 14 Viking-themed cottages near the hotel.

22 Hill Hotel
MAP N3 ▪ Brautarholt 22–24, 105 Reykjavík ▪ 511 3777 ▪ www.22hillhotel.is ▪ ⓀⓀ
Despite the plain exterior, the decent-sized rooms with friendly staff, excellent views, prime location, and good restaurant make this mid-priced option a firm favourite among visitors.

Eyja Guldsmeden Hotel
MAP N3 ▪ Brautarholt 10, 105 Reykjavík ▪ 519 7300 ▪ www.hoteleyja.is ▪ ⓀⓀ
This designer hotel, located just off Laugevegur (the high street), has a commitment to sustainability and offers stylish and contemporary rooms with four-poster beds and slick modcons like flatscreen televisions and fast Wi-Fi.

Hótel Ísland
MAP R4 ▪ Ármúli 9, 108 Reykjavík ▪ 595 7000 ▪ www.hotelisland.is ▪ ⓀⓀ
Centrally located next to the city's financial district, Hótel Ísland is Iceland's first dedicated wellness and medical hotel. It features 129 comfortable rooms, with many offering views of the mountains surrounding Reykjavík. There's also a spa and a bistro serving modern international cuisine.

Hótel Örkin
MAP P4 ▪ Brautarholt 29, 105 Reykjavík ▪ 568 0777 ▪ www.hotelorkin.is ▪ ⓀⓀ
A small budget hotel run by the Faroese

Seamen's Mission, Örkin has a friendly atmosphere. The room prices include breakfast and freshly baked cakes in the afternoon.

Grand Hótel Reykjavík
MAP Q3 ▪ Sigtún 38, 105 Reykjavík ▪ 514 8000 ▪ www.islandshotel.is ▪ ⓀⓀⓀ
Iceland's second largest hotel is situated inside an impressive tower block. It has a modern restaurant and an attractive fitness centre and spa. The conference rooms make it an ideal business venue.

Hilton Reykjavík Nordica
MAP Q4 ▪ Suðurlandsbraut 2, 108 Reykjavík ▪ 444 5000 ▪ www.hiltonreykjavik.com ▪ ⓀⓀⓀ
One of the plushest hotels in the city, Hilton Reykjavik Nordica boasts a great restaurant that offers a delightful fusion of international and Icelandic cuisines. The decor here is distinctly biased towards monochromatic furnishings and pine flooring.

The Retreat at Blue Lagoon
MAP B5 ▪ Nordurljosavegur 11, 240 Grindavík ▪ 420 8700 ▪ www.bluelagoon.com ▪ ⓀⓀⓀ
A modern haven situated in the heart of nature, The Retreat at Blue Lagoon offers 62 luxurious suites, and private thermal spa areas. Floor-to-ceiling windows overlook the surrounding volcanic landscape. The restaurant has a tasting menu.

Hotels Around Iceland

Hótel Búðir
MAP A4 ▪ 356 Snæfellsnes ▪ 435 6700 ▪ www.budir.is ▪ ⓀⓀⓀ

Elegantly refurbished, this hotel is one of Iceland's romantic gems. It has an atmospheric seaside setting, with only a dark wooden church and the nearby white cone of Snæfellsjökull for company. The restaurant is renowned for it's fresh fish and lamb dishes.

Hótel Framtíð
MAP G4 ▪ Vogaland 4, 765 Djúpivogur ▪ 478 8887 ▪ www.hotel framtid.com ▪ ⓀⓀ

This delightful old building overlooks the village harbour of Djúpivogur. There are modern rooms in the main hotel and ordinary wooden cabins for hire, as well as a nearby campsite. The hotel also has a good restaurant.

Hótel Ísafjörður
MAP B2 ▪ Silfurtorg 2, 400 Ísafjörður ▪ 456 4111 ▪ www.hotelisafjordur.is ▪ ⓀⓀ

The solid exterior, providing protection against the severe winter storms, hides a warm and comfortable hotel. The staff are friendly and helpful. The rooms are not huge, but have everything you will need for a night or two. The restaurant is decent, if a bit expensive.

Hótel KEA
MAP E2 ▪ Hafnarstræti 87–89, 600 Akureyri ▪ 460 2000 ▪ www.keahotels.is ▪ ⓀⓀ

Located in the heart of Akureyri, this is the flagship hotel in North Iceland of the KEA chain. The rooms are well furnished and quite spacious. There is a bistro and bar, and the generous buffet breakfast is the ideal start to the day.

Hótel Klaustur
MAP E5 ▪ Klausturvegur 6, 880 Kirkjubæjar klaustur ▪ 487 4900 ▪ www.icelandair hotels.com ▪ ⓀⓀ

It may seem strange to find such a large hotel in such a tiny place, but Hótel Klaustur is well placed for summer excursions to Skaftafell National Park and the Lakagígar craters. Besides its great location, this hotel also offers a decent restaurant and a bar with an outdoor terrace on site, as well as a small heated pool next door.

Hotel Laxá
MAP F2 ▪ Olnbogaas 1, Mývatn ▪ 464 1900 ▪ www.hotellaxa.is ▪ ⓀⓀ

Hotel Laxá features simple but comfortable rooms, some of which have views over Lake Mývatn. The on-site restaurant, Eldey, focuses on locally sourced ingredients and offers a constantly evolving menu. There are also plenty of hiking trails near the hotel.

Hotel Skaftafell
MAP F5 ▪ Freysnes, 785 Öræfi ▪ 478 1945 ▪ www. hotelskaftafell.is ▪ ⓀⓀ

This hotel is a perfectly comfortable base for hiking at nearby Skaftafell National Park. Most of the 63 rooms afford breathtaking glacier views.

Hótel Hamar
MAP B4 ▪ Golfvöllurinn Hamar, 310 Borgarnes ▪ 433 6600 ▪ www.ice landairhotels.com ▪ ⓀⓀ

This long, low hotel in a peaceful setting comes complete with outdoor hot tubs, a top-notch restaurant and an excellent 18-hole golf course. There are great mountain views and each room has a large window and a door opening directly onto the grounds. Do not miss out on a visit to the Borgarnes Settlement Centre during your stay here.

Hótel Hérað
MAP G3 ▪ Miðvangur 5-7, 700 Egilsstaðir ▪ 471 1500 ▪ www. hotelklaustur.is ▪ ⓀⓀ

The bleak, grey exterior of this hotel should not deter you from staying here. Inside, the large rooms are tastefully furnished and another bonus is the helpful staff. Along with the on-site restaurant try Restaurant Nielsen (see p105), located up the road in the oldest house in town.

Leirubakki
MAP D5 ▪ Leirubakki ▪ 487 8700 ▪ www. leirubakki.is ▪ ⓀⓀ

What makes this comfortable, simple modern hotel exceptional is its location in the heart of south Iceland and within sight of the smouldering ridge of Hekla, one of Iceland's most active volcanoes. Guests can enjoy the outdoor natural thermal spring built of lava blocks with beautiful views.

Hótel Rangá

MAP C5 ▪ Ringroad, near Hella ▪ 487 5700 ▪ www.hotelranga.is ▪ ⓚⓚⓚ

This countryside retreat, with 4-star comforts, is especially convenient if salmon fishing on the nearby Rangá river. The lodge-style pine cabins and main buildings are perfectly decorated and there is an excellent restaurant. As well as the river, it is also close to all of south Iceland's best attractions.

Guesthouses

Galleri Laugarvatn

MAP C5 ▪ Laugarvatn ▪ 847 0805 ▪ www.galleri laugarvatn.is ▪ ⓚ

Run by a husband and wife team, Galleri Laugarvatn started life as a design and crafts store before it became a bright and cheerful bed and breakfast. It has five rooms, three of which have shared bathrooms. Rooms are bright, clean and tastefully appointed, and there's a charming café on site.

Gistiheimilið Baldursbrá

MAP L4 ▪ Laufásvegur 41, 101 Reykjavík ▪ 552 6646 ▪ ⓚ

Located in a residential area, this family-run place provides spacious rooms with shared bathrooms and an outdoor hot tub for a very reasonable price.

Gistiheimilið Hamar

MAP C6 ▪ Herjólfsgata 4, Heimaey, Vestmannaeyjar ▪ 481 3400 ▪ Open May–Sep ▪ www.guesthouse hamar.is ▪ ⓚ

This modern block near the harbour has large rooms that sleep up to four guests, with private bathrooms. Breakfast is available for patrons.

Gistiheimilið Sunna

MAP M3 ▪ Þórsgata 26, 101 Reykjavík ▪ 511 5570 ▪ www.sunna.is ▪ ⓚ

Close to Hallgrímskirkja, this guesthouse offers clean rooms with access to a kitchenette, and shared or private bathrooms. A buffet breakfast is included. Some rooms have views over the neighbouring church.

Kex Hostel

MAP B5 ▪ Skúlagata 28, 101 Reykjavík ▪ 561 6060 ▪ www.kexhostel.is ▪ ⓚ

Vibrant and colourful, Kex Hostel is housed inside a renovated biscuit factory. It has comfortable dorms for up to 16 people as well as private rooms. The decor is welcoming with vintage furniture dotted around the spacious lobby and an on-site gastropub.

Lava Hostel

MAP B5 ▪ Hjallabraut 51, 220 Hafnarfjörður ▪ 565 0900 ▪ www.lavahostel.is ▪ ⓚ

This simple, self-catering guesthouse has two to eight beds per room, shared bathrooms and full kitchen facilities. There is also a dormitory with sleeping-bag accommodation (bring your own or rent linen here). Buses to Reykjavík, and the international airport, stop nearby.

Skálholtsskóli

MAP C5 ▪ Skálholt ▪ 486 8870 ▪ www.skalholt.is ▪ ⓚ

The guesthouse is attached to the Skálholt Center – a historic cultural venue run by the Evangelical Lutheran Church of Iceland. Summer concerts at the cathedral are a bonus. Besides double and single rooms, Skálholtsskóli also offers sleeping bag services. Book in advance.

Sólheimar Eco-Village

MAP C5 ▪ Grímsnes, 801 Selfoss ▪ 480 4483 ▪ www.solheimar.is ▪ ⓚ

A stay in this world renowned sustainable community, founded in 1930, is an unforgettable experience. As well as the comfortable guesthouse with access to a swimming pool and hot tub, there are crafts workshops, a café and a sculpture garden.

Gistiheimilið Hof

MAP A4 ▪ Hofgarðar, 365 Snæfellsbær ▪ 846 3897 ▪ www.gistihof.is ▪ ⓚⓚ

Long, turf-roofed building in a panoramic rural location near to a sandy beach. The guesthouse has six self-contained units, with three double bedrooms, a bathroom, kitchenette and outdoor hot tub. There are 16 en-suite rooms available in the summer.

Gistihúsið Egilsstöðum

MAP G3 ▪ Egilsstaðir ▪ 471 1114 ▪ www.lake hotel.is ▪ ⓚⓚ

With a cosy family-run atmosphere this comfortable hotel is set in a large renovated farmhouse just outside of town and with great views over the lake. Rooms are all en-suite. There is a great restaurant, Eldhúsið, on the first floor and a spa, Baðhúsið, on the ground floor.

For a key to hotel price categories see p128

Hotel Geysir

MAP C5 ■ Haukadalur 35, 806 Selfoss ■ 480 6800 ■ www.hotelgeysir.is ■ ⓚⓚ

Located just opposite the geothermal springs, Litli Geysir is a great choice for group accommodation. The hotel offers 22 rooms with the breakfast included in the price. They have a telescope in the lounge and the adjoining Geysir Centre has a café and two restaurants.

Puffin Hotel Vík

MAP D6 ■ Vikurbraut 26, Vík ■ 467 1212 ■ www.puffinhotelvik.is ■ ⓚⓚ

Both a charming hotel and hostel, Puffin has 22 en-suite rooms set between a modern building and an older wing. A separate hostel building offers 12 cheaper rooms in various sizes with cooking facilities and shared bathrooms. You also have the option of staying in one of the apartments.

Summer Hotels and Eddas

Hólar í Hjaltadal

MAP D2 ■ Hólar, near Sauðárkrókur ■ 849 6348 ■ Open Jun–Aug ■ www.visitholar.is ■ ⓚ

The small community of Hólar is home to a historically important cathedral, the island's largest estate and Hólar University, where student accommodation is available to tourists.

Hótel Edda Höfn

MAP G5 ■ Höfn ■ 444 4850 ■ Open May–Sep ■ www.icelandairhotels.com ■ ⓚ

Well placed for glacier trips to Vatnajökull or

hiking in the Lónsöræfi reserve, these school buildings offer 36 newly restored rooms with private bathrooms and toilets, plus a restaurant that serves breakfast.

Hótel Hallormstaður

MAP G3 ■ Hallormstaður, near Egilsstaðir ■ 471 2400 ■ www.701hotels.is ■ ⓚ

Cosy country hotel set inside Iceland's most extensive forest, close to Lagarfljót. The hotel has self-contained wooden cottages, rooms in a large guesthouse and summer-only accommodation. Guests can choose between two restaurants.

Hotel Skógar

MAP C6 ■ Skógum, 861 Hvolsvöllur ■ 487 4880 ■ www.hotelskogar.is ■ ⓚ

A small and cosy hotel, with 12 rooms in single, double, triple standard and deluxe categories, plus a hot tub and sauna. It's located just a few minutes walk from Skógafoss waterfall and the Skógar Museum.

Fosshotel Húsavík

MAP E2 ■ Ketilsbraut 22, 640 Húsavík ■ 464 1220 ■ www.fosshotel.is ■ ⓚⓚ

Located close to Husavik's harbour, Fosshotel Húsavík is the largest business hotel in North Iceland. It has over 100 rooms which are spacious, smartly furnished and are equipped with satellite TVs, fridge, minibars and Wi-Fi. The menu at its Moby Dick restaurant uses mostly local ingredients. The

hotel also offers free parking facility for guests.

Fosshótel Vatnajökull

MAP G5 ■ Route 1 near Höfn, Hornafjörður ■ 478 2555 ■ www.fosshotel.is ■ ⓚⓚ

This is a functional, tidy place, with warm but small and simply furnished rooms. Given the fantastic location, you should get a room with glacier views. There is also an on-site restaurant.

Hótel Aldan

MAP H3 ■ Norðurgata 2, 710 Seyðisfjörður ■ 472 1277 ■ www.hotelaldan.is ■ ⓚⓚ

A 19th-century wooden building by the harbour, this was once a bank but has now been converted into a nine-bedroom hotel, which retains a historic atmosphere with period furnishings. There is a bar and an excellent restaurant. More rooms are available in the nearby sister operation, Hótel Snæfell, which is run by the same family.

Hótel Edda Ísafjörður

MAP B2 ■ Torfnes, Ísafjörður ■ 444 4960 ■ Open Jun–Aug ■ www.icelandairhotels.com ■ ⓚⓚ

Located near the centre of Ísafjörður, this school (for most of the year) has good facilities. Rooms have en-suite bathrooms or in-room washbasins. There is a campsite and sleeping-bag space in the heated sports hall. Buffet breakfast is available.

Hótel Flókalundur
MAP C5 ■ Vatnsfirði, 451 Patreksfjörður ■ 456 2011 ■ Open May–Sep ■ www.flokalundur.is ■ ⓀⓀ
A family-run hotel, Flókalundur is located on the south coast of the Westfjords, within striking distance of Látrabjarg, Rauðasandur and Ísafjörður. The hotel has 15 comfortable rooms with spectacular views of the surrounding landscape.

Campsites and Character Stays

Egilsstaðir Campsite
MAP G3 ■ Kaupvangur 17, 700 Egilsstaðir ■ 470 0750 ■ www.campegliss tadir.is ■ Ⓚ
Well-situated in the middle of Egilsstaðir, this newly renovated campsite offers 24-hour facilities including modern bathrooms, washing machines, and a sheltered barbecue and seating area. Appliances such as an electric stove and grill, a toaster, a microwave and a kettle are also available for visitors.

Galtalækur II
MAP C5 ■ Route 26, Rangárþing ytra, Hella ■ 487 6528 ■ www.1.is/gl2/en ■ Ⓚ
Galtalækur II offers a pleasant campsite and self-contained cabins near Tangavatn lake, Þjófafoss waterfall and Hekla volcano. You can buy fishing licences here.

Hamrar Campsite
MAP E2 ■ Kjarnaskógur, Akureyri ■ 461 2264 ■ www.hamrar.is ■ Ⓚ
Enormous camping grounds near woodland outside Akureyri in the north of the island. You

do not need to reserve a space in advance. There are toilets, hot showers, washing machines and tumble dryers on site, along with a kitchen and a covered dining area.

Hlíð Campsite
MAP F2 ■ Reykjahlíð, Mývatn ■ 464 4103 ■ www.myvatnaccom modation.is ■ Ⓚ
This is a great place to base yourself while at Mývatn; there are superb views over Reykjahlíð and the lake. The site offers hot showers, toilets and outdoor sinks for washing plates and cutlery. Wooden cabins and a dorm building are also available.

Hótel Dyrhólaey
MAP D6 ■ Near Vík ■ 487 1333 ■ www.dyrholaey.is ■ Ⓚ
This lakeside farmstead is nestled in the hills above Dyrhólaey bird reserve. The fully equipped rooms come complete with private bathrooms and are clean, warm and very comfortable. North facing rooms have good views of the Mýrdalsjökull icecap. Staff are helpful and the restaurant offers a healthy breakfast and good-value evening buffet of Icelandic dishes.

Reykjavík Campsite
MAP R2 ■ Sundlaugavegur 34, 105 Reykjavík ■ 568 6944 ■ www.reykjavik campsite.is ■ Ⓚ
The huge grassy slope of this campsite has room for hundreds of tents. A 35-40-minute walk from the city centre, the site has a covered cooking area, washing machine, tumble dryer, toilets and showers.

Hótel Anna
MAP D6 ■ Moldnúpur, Route 246, between Skógar and Seljarlandsfoss ■ 487 8950 ■ www.hotel anna.is ■ ⓀⓀ
Cosy farmhouse in a great rural location with Eyjafjallajökull rising above it. Large beds, low ceilings and old wooden furniture add to the character. Price includes use of hot tubs and sauna.

Hótel Laki
MAP E5 ■ Efri Vík, Kirkjubæjarklaustur ■ 412 4600 ■ www.hotellaki.is ■ ⓀⓀⓀ
A converted farmhouse, the rooms at this family-run hotel are all en-suite doubles. Located on the edge of a pseudocrater and a lava field stretching to Lakagígar, Hótel Laki is the perfect base for hikers and nature lovers.

Hótel Látrabjarg
MAP A2 ■ On Route 615 and 3 km (1.9 miles) from the junction of 612/615 in Vesturbyggð ■ 456 1500 ■ Open mid-May–Sep ■ www.latrabjarg.com ■ ⓀⓀⓀ
Originally a boarding school, this hotel is close to the beach and bird cliffs. Rooms have en-suite bathrooms. Freshwater trout fishing is possible in the nearby Sauðlauksdalur lake for a small fee.

Hótel Tindastóll
MAP D2 ■ Lindargata 3, Sauðárkrókur ■ 453 5002 ■ www.arctichotels.is ■ ⓀⓀⓀⓀ
Iceland's oldest hotel opened in 1884 and has an outdoor spa. Rooms have a warm and cosy feel. A resident ghost adds to the atmosphere.

For a key to hotel price categories see p128

General Index

Page numbers in **bold** refer to Top 10 Highlights.

12 Tónar 75

A

Accommodation 127, 128–33
  campsites 133
  character stays 133
  guesthouses 131–2
  hotels 128–31
  summer hotels and Eddas 132–3
Air travel 67, 120, 121
Akranes 85
Akranes Museum Centre 85, 86
Akureyrarkirkja (Akureyri) 96
Akureyri 7, 96
  accommodation 130, 133
  restaurants 62, 99
Alcohol 67, 122–3
Aldeyjarfoss 45, 117
Almannagjá 12, 108
Alþing 12, 13, 36
Alþingishúsið (Parliament House) (Reykjavík) 75, 78
Arason, Bishop Jón 36, 37, 39, 70, 96
Árbær Open Air Museum (Reykjavík) 41, 54
Arctic Circle 95
Arctic foxes 50, 90
Arnarson, Ingólfur 36, 37, 51, 75
Arnarstapi 27, 54
Árnason, Kristinn 69
Ásbyrgi 24, 54
Askja 21, 47, 102, 117
  trips and tours 126, 127
Ásmundur Sveinsson Sculpture Museum (Reykjavík) 41, 78
Atlavík 101, 103
Aurora borealis see Northern lights
Avalanches 123

B

Bænahús church (Núpsstaður) 38
Bakkagerði see Borgarfjörður Eystri
Banks 124
Bárður's statue 27
Barnafoss 44, 83, 85

Bars and pubs 60–61
  Reykjavík 80
Bathing 53
  see also Hot springs; Swimming
Beachcombing 59
Beaches 67
Beast of Hvalfjörður 59
Bergþór 59
Berries 66
Berserkjahraun lava field 86
Birds 50–51
  bird watching 67
  Brieðafjörður 51
  Dyrhólaey 50
  Eyjabakkar 104
  Garðskagi 51
  Grótta 66
  Héraðsflói 103
  Höfði Nature Park 97
  Hornabjarg 50
  Ingólfshöfði 51
  Jökulsá á Dal 51
  Jökulsárlón 33, 50
  Látrabjarg bird cliffs 11, **28–9**, 50
  Mývatn 20
  offshore islands 70–71
  Snæfellskökull National Park 27
  Tjörnin 58
  Vatnajökull 24
Bjargtangar 29
Bjarnarfell 17
Björk 43, 69
Björnsson, Sveinn 37
Bláhnúkur 30, 31
Blesi 16
Blönduós 95
  restaurants 99
Blue Lagoon 5, 10, **14–15**, 48, 109
  bathing 53
  itineraries 6, 7
Boat trips, Jökulsárlón 33
Bolungarvík 92
Borg á Mýrum 86
Borgarfjörður Eystri 100, 102
  restaurants 105
Borgarnes 82, 85
  accommodation 130
  restaurants 87
  swimming 53
Borgarnes Settlement Center 42, 58, 83, 85
Breiðárlón 32

Breiðavík 29, 50
Bridge between continents 112
Brieðafjörður 51, 84
Búðir 82, 84
  restaurants 87
Bus travel 120, 121
  passes 67, 120
Bustarfell 104

C

Cafés 60–61
  Reykjavík 80
Camping 67, 127, 133
Canyons and gorges
  Ásbyrgi 24
  Gullfoss 18
  Jökulsárgljúfur 22–3, 25, 97
  Pennugil 92
Car travel 120–21
Caves
  Vatnshellir lava cave 84
  Víðgelmir Cave 86
Children's activities 58–9
Christianity 36
Churches 38–9
  Akureyrarkirkja 96
  Bænahús (Núpsstaður) 38
  Búðir Church 82, 84
  Dómkirkjan (Reykjavík) 38
  Grund Church 38
  Hallgrímskirkja (Reykjavík) 6, 38–9, 76, 77
  Haukadlur Church 17
  Hóladómkirkja (Hólar) 39, 96
  Landakotskirkja (Reykjavík) 38
  Skálholtskirkja 39
  Strandarkirkja (Selvogur) 39
  Stykkishólmur Church 86
  Valþjófsstaður 103, 104
  Víðimýri 39
  Vík Church 4
  Þingeyrakirkja 39, 98
  Þingvellir Church 12, 108
Clubs 60–61
Continental plates 112
COVID-19 125
Credit cards 124
Crime 123
Crowberries 66
Customs 122, 123
Cycling 67, 121

D

Dalvík, festivals 68–9
Deildartunguhver 48, 85
Denmark 36
Dermatology 14
Dettifoss 22–3, 25, 44, 97
Dhoon 29, 92
Dimmuborgir 20, 97
Djasshátíð – Reykjavík Jazz
  Festival 69
Djúpalónssandur 26
Djúpavík 92
  restaurants 93
Djúpivogur 4, 43, 104
  accommodation 130
  restaurants 105
Dómkirkjan (Reykjavík) 38
Drangajökull 91
Drangey 71
Dritvík 26
Driving 120–21
  Highland 116
Drugs 122–3
Dynjandi 45, 90, 91
Dyrhólaey 50
  accommodation 133

E

East Iceland 100–5
  A Day in East Iceland 103
  map 100
  restaurants 105
  sights 100–4
Edda hotels 127, 132–3
Eggs, bird 28
Egil's Saga 42, 58, 84
Egilsstaðir 7, 101, 103
  accommodation 130,
    131, 133
  restaurants 105
Einar Jónsson Sculpture
  Museum (Reykjavík) 40, 78
Einarsson, Bishop Gissur 36
Eirik the Red 86
Eiríksson, Leifur 37, 76
Eiríksstaðir (Búðardalur)
  86
Eldey 71
Eldfell 47, 110
Electrical appliances 124
Eliasson, Olafur 77
Emergency services 123
Esja, Mount 54, 118–19
Eyjabakkar 104
Eyjafjallajökull 4, 7, 44,
  46, 54
Eyrarbakki 111, 112
  restaurants 113
Eyrbyggja Saga 83, 86
Eyvindur 59

F

Farm holidays 127
Ferries 120, 121
Festivals 68–9
Film locations 33
Fimmvörðuháls trail 54, 116
Finnbogadóttir, Vigdís 37
Fish 63
Fishing 52
Fiskidagurinn Mikli (Dalvík)
  68–9
Fjallsárlón 25
Flash floods 25
Flatey 71, 84
Fljótshlíð 110
Flóklandur 88, 89, 91
Flora
  Landmannalaugar 31
  wild flowers 55
  Þingvellir 13
Folktales 59
Food and drink
  dining 126, 127
  drinking 122–3
  Top 10 foods 63
  see also Bars and pubs;
    Cafés; Restaurants
Free attractions 66–7
Frostastaðavatn 31, 117
Fuel 121

G

Gamla Pakkhúsið (Ólafsvík)
  86
Garðskagi 51
Geothermal power 15, 42–3
Geysers *see* Hot springs
  and geysers
Geysir 16, 48, 111
Geysir Centre 17
Geysir Hot Springs area 6,
  10, **16–17**, 109
  accommodation 131
  restaurants 113
Glaciation 24
Glanni 86
Glaumbær 98
Glymur 44, 85
Goðafoss 45, 98
Golden Circle 108–9, 111,
  126, 127
Gorbachev, Mikhail 78
Gorges *see* Canyons and
  gorges
Government advice 122
Grenjaðarstaður 98
Grettir's Saga 95, 96
Grettislaug 53
Grímsey 71, 95
Grímsvötn 47

Grjótagjá 66, 97
Grótta 66
Grund Church 38
Guano 29
Guesthouses 67, 131–2
Gullfoss 6, 10, **18–19**, 44,
  109, 111
  restaurants 113
Gunnarsson, Gunnar 101

H

Hælavíkurbjarg 92
Hafnarfjörður (Reykjavík) 78
Hafragilsfoss 97
Hafsteinn, Hannes 37
Halla 59
Hallgrímskirkja (Reykjavík)
  6, 38–9, 76, 77
Hallgrímsson, Jónas 37, 95
Hallormsstaður 101, 103
  accommodation 132
Harpa (Reykjavík) 6, 56–7,
  76–7
Haukadalur Forest 17
Haukadlur Church 17
Health 122, 123
  Blue Lagoon clinics 14
Heiðmörk Park 55
Heimaey 47, 71, 110
  accommodation 131
Hekla, Mount 31, 46, 112,
  115, 117
Hellnar 26, 54
Hengifoss 103, 104
Hengill 49
Héraðsflói 103
Herðubreið 117
Herring Era Museum
  (Siglufjörður) 42
The Highland Interior 114–17
  A Day in the Highlands 117
  map 114
  sights 114–17
Hiking 52, 66, 121
  Arnarstapi to Hellnar 54
  Ásbyrgi 54
  Esja 54
  Fimmvörðuháls 54
  Heiðmörk Park 55
  Hveragerði 111, 112
  Landmannalaugar 31
  Laugavegur 5, 30, 31, 55,
    115
  safety 123
  Snæfellsjökull National
    Park 27
  Svartifoss 54
  trails 54–5
  Þingvellir 54
  Þórsmörk 55, 115, 116

History, Moments in 36–7
Hjálmtýsdóttir, Sigrún 69
Hnjótur Museum 29
Höfði House (Reykjavík) 77, 78
Höfði Nature Park 97
Höfn 7, 103
  accommodation 132
  restaurants 62, 105
Hofsós 42, 53, 98
Hóladómkirkja (Hólar) 39, 96
Hólar 96
Hólmavík Museum of Sorcery and Witchcraft 90
Holuhraun 67
Hornabjarg 50
Horse riding 52, 58, 126
Hostels 67, 127
Hot springs and geysers 48–9
  Blesi 16
  Blue Lagoon 10, **14–15**, 48, 53, 109
  Deildartunguhver 48, 85
  Geysir 16, 48, 111
  Geysir Hot Springs area 6, 10, **16–17**, 109
  Grettislaug 53
  Grjótagjá 66, 97
  Hengill 49
  Hveravellir 49
  Jarðböðin Nature Baths 7, 21, 48, 53, 97
  Konungshver 16
  Krossneslaug 53
  Landmannalaugar 30, 48, 53, 66
  Litli Geysir 16
  Námaskarð 7, 21, 49
  natural thermal pools 66, 126
  Nauthólsvík Geothermal Beach (Reykjavík) 78
  Seltún 15, 49
  Strokkur 6, 16, 49, 109
Hotels 127
  around Iceland 130–1
  character stays 133
  Reykjavík 128–9
  summer hotels and Eddas 132–3
Hrafnseyri 90, 91
Hrafntinnusker 31
Hraun í Öxnadalur 95
Hraunfossar 44, 83, 85
Hrísey 70
Húsafell 86
Húsavík 7, 43, 96
  restaurants 99

Húsavík Whale Museum 43, 58, 96
Hvalfjörður 85
  restaurants 87
Hvallátur 92
Hvannadalshnjúkur 24
Hveragerði 111, 112
Hveravellir 49, 115
Hverfjall 21, 97
Hvítserkur (East Iceland) 104
Hvítserkur (North Iceland) 98
Hvolsvöllur Saga Centre 6, 112

I

Icebergs (Jökulsárlón) 5, 7, 10, 32, 111
Icecaps
  Drangajökull 91
  Eyjafjallajökull 4, 7, 44, 46, 54
  Höfsjökull 19
  Langjökull 19, 115, 116
  Mýrdalsjökull 47, 54, 55, 112
  Snæfellsjökull 26, 27, 46, 82, 84
  Vatnajökull 7, 11, 24, 32, 101
Icecaves 33
Icelandic Emigration Centre (Hofsós) 42, 98
Icelandic Museum of Rock & Roll (Reykjanesbær) 43
ID 123
Imagine Peace Tower (Viðey) 70, 78
Independence 37
Ingólfshöfði 51
Insurance 122, 123
Ísafjörður 43, 88, 91
  accommodation 130, 132
  restaurants 62, 93
Íslandi, Stefán 69
Islands, offshore 70–1
  Drangey 71
  Eldey 71
  Flatey 71, 84
  Grímsey 71, 95
  Heimaey 47, 71, 110
  Hrísey 70
  Lundey 70
  Papey 71
  Surtsey 71, 110
  Vestmannaeyjar 110
  Viðey 70
  Vigur 70
  Westman Islands 71

Itineraries
  A Day in East Iceland 103
  A Day in the Highlands 117
  A Day in the Lake Mývatn Area 97
  A Day in Reykjavík 77
  A Day in South Iceland 111
  A Day in the West 85
  A Day in the Westfjords 91
  Seven Days in Iceland 6–7
  Two Days in Iceland 6
  see also Trips and tours

J

Jazz 68
Jeep touring 52
Jökulhlaups 25, 47
Jökulsá á Dal 51
Jökulsárgljúfur 22–3, 25, 97
Jökulsárlón 8–9, 11, **32–3**, 111
  itineraries 7
  wildlife 50
Jónsson, Einar 40, 78
Jónsson, Ríkarður 43
Jónsson, Samúel 92

K

Kaldalón 92
Kaldidalur 83, 85
Kalmar Union 36
Kárahnjúkar hydro dam 103, 104
Katla 47, 112
Keldur farm 117
Kerið crater 6, 111, 112
Kerlingarfjall 86
Kirkjubæjarklaustur 106–7, 111
  accommodation 130, 133
  Chamber Music Festival 69
Kirkjugólf 106–7, 111
Kjarval, Jóhannes 40
Kjarvalsstaðir (Reykjavík Art Museum) 6, 40, 76
The Kjölur Route 19, 115, 116
KK 69
Konungshver 16
Krafla 7, 21, 47
Krafla Fires 21, 47
Krossneslaug 53

L

Lagarfljót lake 100, 101, 103
Lakagígar 25, 37, 46, 116
  trips and tours 126, 127

Lake Mývatn 7, 10, **20–21**, 97
A Day in the Lake Mývatn
  Area 97
accommodation 130, 133
restaurants 99
wildlife 50
Landakotskirkja (Reykjavík)
  38
Landmannalaugar area 5,
  11, **30–31**
bathing 48, 53
highland landscape
  72–3, 115, 117
Landnámssýningin
  (Settlement Exhibition)
  (Reykjavík) 6, 40, 75, 77
Langabúð (Djúpivogur) 43
Langisjór 115
Langjökull 19, 115, 116
Language 126
Látrabjarg bird cliffs 11,
  28–9, 89
bird watching 50
Laufás 98
Laugardalur Park and
  Recreation Area
  (Reykjavík) 6, 53, 77
Laugarvatn 53, 111
accommodation 133
Laugavegur 5, 30, 31, 55, 115
Lava Centre 112
Laxá í Aðaldal 20, 98
Laxárdalur 5, 84–5
Laxdæla Saga 5, 84
Laxness, Halldór 111
Leirhnjúkur 97
Leirubakki 112, 117
accommodation 130–31
Lennon, John 70, 78
LGBTQ+ travel 123
Lighthouses
Akranes 85
Bjargtangar 29
Garðskagi 51
Listasafn Íslands (National
  Gallery) (Reykjavík) 6, 40,
  75
Ljótipollur 31
Lögberg 12
Lögurinn lake 103
Lónsöræfi 104
Lundey 70
Lutheran Church 36–7

M

Maps
East Iceland 100
Highland Interior 114
itineraries 6–7
North Iceland 94–5

Maps (cont.)
Reykjavík 74–5
South Iceland 108–9
West Iceland and the
  Snæfellsnes Peninsula
  82–3
Westfjords 88–9
Margrete, Queen of
  Denmark 36
Menningarnótt (Reykjavík)
  68
Midtown (Reykjavík) 75
Mjóifjörður 102
Mobile phones 124
Money 124
Money-saving tips 67
Mountain guides 126, 127
Mugison 69
Museums and galleries
  40–3
Akranes Folk Museum
  85, 86
Árbær Open Air museum
  (Reykjavík) 41, 58
Ásmundur Sveinsson
  Sculpture Museum
  (Reykjavík) 41, 78
Borgarnes Settlement
  Center 42, 58, 83
Einar Jónsson Sculpture
  Museum (Reykjavík)
  40, 78
Geysir Centre 17
Herring Era Museum
  (Siglufjörður) 42
Hnjótur Museum 29
Hólmavík Museum
  of Sorcery and Witchcraft
  90
Húsavík Whale Museum
  43, 58, 96
Hvolsvöllur Saga Centre
  6, 112
Icelandic Emigration
  Centre (Hofsós) 42, 98
Icelandic Museum of
  Rock & Roll
  (Reykjanesbær) 43
Icelandic Saltfish
  Museum (Grindavík) 15
Kjarvalsstaðir (Reykjavík
  Art Museum) 6, 40, 76
Landnámssýningin
  (Settlement Exhibition)
  (Reykjavík) 6, 40, 75, 77
Lava Centre 112
Langabúð (Djúpivogur) 43
Listasafn Íslands
  National Gallery
  (Reykjavík) 40, 75

Museums and galleries
  (cont.)
Orka Náttúrinnar
  Geothermal Energy
  Exhibition 42–3
Reykjavík Maritime
  Museum 41
Safnahúsið (Reykjavík) 6,
  75, 77
Saga Museum
  (Reykjavík) 41, 58,
  75
Sigurjón Ólafsson
  Sculpture Museum
  (Reykjvík) 41, 78
Skógar Museum 42
Snorrastofa (Reykholt)
  83
Viking World
  (Reykjanesbær) 43
Westfjords Maritime
  Museum (Ísafjörður)
  43, 91
Þjóðminjasafn Íslands
  (National Museum)
  (Reykjavík) 40, 76, 77
Music
festivals 68, 69
top musicians 69
Mýrdalsjökull 47, 54, 55,
  112
Myrkir Músikdagar
  (Reykjavík) 69
Mývatn Nature Baths 7,
  21, 48, 53, 97

N

Naddoður 36
Námaskarð 7, 21, 49,
  97
National parks
Snæfellsjökull National
  Park 11, **26–7**, 84
Vatnajökull National
  Park 7, 11, **24–5**, 101
Þingvellir National
  Park 10, **12–13**, 54,
  67, 108
Natural hazards 123
Nauthólsvík Geothermal
  Beach (Reykjavík) 78
Njál's Saga 84, 110
Norðurfjörður 91
Norræna Húsið 78
North Iceland 94–9
A Day in the Lake Mývatn
  Area 97
map 94–5
restaurants 99
sights 94–8

Northern lights 5, 34–5, 66
  watching 53
Norway 36
Núpsstaður 38

O
Óðinn 41
Ófærufoss 30, 45
Off-season, travelling 67
Ólafsson, Sigurjón 41, 78
Ólafur Tryggvason, King of
  Norway 36
Opening hours 125
Öræfajökull 46
Orka Náttúrinnar
  Geothermal Energy
  Exhibition 42–3
Ormurinn 59
Öskjuhlíð hill (Reykjavík)
  66, 74, 77
Outdoor activities 52–3
Öxara river 108
Öxarárfoss 13, 59

P
Papey 71
Parks and gardens
  Heiðmörk Park 55
  Laugardalur Park and
    Recreation Area
    (Reykjavík) 6, 53, 77
  Reykjavík Botanic
    Gardens 58–9
  Skrúður 92
Passports 122
Patreksfjörður 89
  accommodation 133
  restaurants 93
Peningagjá 13
Pennugil 92
Perlan (Reykjavík) 6, 77
Personal security 123
Pharmacies 122
Police 123
Postal services 124, 125
Pseudocraters 20, 97, 111
Pubs see Bars and pubs
Puffins 51, 70, 71
  Látrabjarg bird cliffs 28
  puffin watching 126, 127

R
Ráðhúsið (Reykjavík)
  67, 77
Rauðasandur 89
Rauðhólar 94, 97
Reagan, Ronald 78
Reiðskörð 92
Reindeer 51, 67
Religion 36–7

Restaurants 126, 127
  Blue Lagoon 15
  cheaper eats in
    Reykjavík 64–5
  East Iceland 105
  fine dining 62–3
  North Iceland 99
  Reykjavík 81
  smoking in 122
  South Iceland 113
  West Iceland and the
    Snæfellsnes Peninsula 87
  Westfjords 93
Reykholt 83
  restaurants 87
Reykjadalur 55
Reykjanes 92
Reykjanesbær 43
Reykjavík 5, 74–81
  A Day in Reykjavík 77
  accommodation 128–9,
    131–2, 133
  bars, clubs and cafés in
    Reykjavík 60–61, 80
  churches 38–9
  festivals 68–9
  history 36
  itineraries 6, 7, 77
  map 74–5
  museums and galleries
    40–41
  restaurants 62–5, 81
  shopping 79
  sights 74–8
Reykjavík Art Museum see
  Kjarvalsstaðir
Reykjavík Arts Festival 40,
  68
Reykjavík Botanic Gardens
  58–9
Reykjavík Harbour 58, 75
Reykjavík International
  Film Festival (RIFF) 68
Reykjavík Maritime
  Museum 41
Reykjavík Pride 69
Ringroad 33
River rafting 52
Road travel 120–21
  Highland driving 116

S
Sæmundur the Wise 59
Safety 122, 123
Safnahúsið 6, 75, 77
Saga Museum 41, 58, 75
Sargon 29
Sauðárkrókur 95
  accommodation 132, 133
Scale Model of Iceland 67

Scuba diving 53
Sea travel 120
Seals 50, 59, 67, 111
Selárdalslaug 53
Selárdalur 92
Selatangar 15
Self-catering 67, 127
Selfoss 6, 111
  accommodation 131
  restaurants 113
Seljalandsfoss 7, 44, 67
Seljavallalaug 112
Seltún 15, 49
Seyðisfjörður 7, 102
  accommodation 132
  restaurants 105
Shipwrecks 29, 59, 92
Shopping 126
  Reykjavík 79
Siglufjörður 42
  festivals 69
Sigmundsson, Kristinn 69
Sigríðarstofa trail (Gullfoss)
  19
Sigur Rós 43, 69
Sigurðardóttir, Jóhanna 37
Sigurðsson, Jón 37, 90
Sigurjón Ólafsson
  Sculpture Museum 41,
  78
Síldarævintýri (Siglufjörður)
  69
Skaftafell 7, 25
  accommodation 130
Skálholt 111
  guesthouses 131
Skálholtskirkja 39
Skallagrímsson, Egill 82,
  83, 84, 86
Skeiðarárjökull 47
Skiing 53
Skjaldbreiður 12, 108
Skjálfandi 50
Skógafoss 7, 45, 59
Skógar, accommodation
  132
Skógar Museum 42
Skriðuklaustur 100, 101, 103
  restaurants 105
Skrúður 92
Skútustaðir 97
  accommodation 130
Smoking 122–3
Snæfell 46, 103, 104
Snæfellsbær,
  accommodation 131–2
Snæfellsjökull 26, 27, 46,
  82, 84
Snæfellsjökull National
  Park 11, **26–7**, 84

Snæfellsnes Peninsula 26, 82, 84
accommodation 130
restaurants 87
see also West Iceland and the Snæfellsnes Peninsula
Snorrastofa (Reykholt) 83
Snorri 59
Snowboarding 53
Snowmobiling 52
South Iceland 108–13
A Day in South Iceland 111
map 108–9
restaurants 113
sights 108–12
Spas, Blue Lagoon 14
Sports *see* Outdoor activities
Sprengisandur Route 117
Steinasafn Petru 104
Stokkseyri 111, 112
restaurants 63
Stórutjarnir, accommodation 132
Strandarkirkja
church 39
restaurants 65
Strandir coast 88, 90, 92
Strokkur 6, 16, 49, 109
Sturluson, Snorri 37, 41, 82
Stykkishólmur 83
church 86
restaurants 87
Súðavík Arctic Fox Centre 90–1
Summer hotels 127, 132–3
Surtsey 71, 110
Sustainable Travel 125
Svartfoss 7, 25
hiking trail 54
Svartsengi Geothermal Power Station 14, 15
Sveinsson, Ásmundur 41, 78
Swimming 52, 58, 126
public pools 67, 126
safety 123
top places for 53
see also Hot springs

T
Tax refunds 67, 126
Taxis 121
Time zone 124
Tjörnes 98
Tjörnin (Reykjavík) 58, 77, 78
Tómasdóttir, Sigríður, plaque to 19
Torrini, Emiliana 69
Transport 120–21

Travellers with specific requirements 124
Trips and tours 126, 127
Trolls 59

V
Vaglaskógur 98
Valþjófsstaður 103, 104
VAT 126
Vatnajökull 7, 11, 24, 32, 101
Vatnajökull National Park 7, 11, **24–5**, 101
accommodation 132
Vatnshellir lava cave 84
Veiðivötn 115
Verne, Jules 27
Vestmannaeyjar 110
Viðey 70, 78
Víðgelmir Cave 86
Víðimýri chapel 39
Vigur 70
Vík 7, 110–11
church 4
Viking World (Reykjanesbær) 43
Vikings 36
Vilgerðarson, Flóki 36, 37, 89
Visas 122, 123
Visitor Information 125
Víti crater 21, 97, 102
Volcanoes 46–7
Askja 21, 47, 102, 117, 126, 127
Eldfell 47, 110
Eyjafjallajökull 4, 7, 46
Grímsvötn 47
Hekla 31, 46, 112, 115, 117
Inside the Volcano tour 112
Katla 47, 112
Krafla 7, 21, 47, 67
Lakagígar 25, 37, 46, 116
Öræfajökull 46
Skjaldbreiður 12, 108
Snæfell 46, 103, 104
Vopnafjörður 100, 102
restaurants 105

W
Walking 121
Waterfalls 44–5, 67
Aldeyjarfoss 45, 117
Barnafoss 44, 83, 85
Dettifoss 22–3, 25, 44, 97
Dynjandi 45, 90
Glanni 86
Glymur 44, 85
Goðafoss 45, 98
Gullfoss 10, **18–19**, 44, 109, 111
Hafragilsfoss 97

Waterfalls (cont.)
Hengifoss 103, 104
Hraunfossar 44, 83, 85
Ófærufoss 30, 45
Öxarárfoss 13, 59
Seljalandsfoss 7, 44, 67
Skógafoss 7, 45, 59
Svartfoss 7, 25, 54
Weather 124, 125
Were-seals 59
West Iceland and the Snæfellsnes Peninsula 82–7
A Day in the West 85
map 82–3
restaurants 87
sights 82–6
Westfjords 88–93
A Day in the Westfjords 91
map 88–9
restaurants 93
sights 88–92
Westfjords Maritime Museum (Ísafjörður) 43, 91
Westman Islands 71
Whales
Húsavík Whale Museum 43, 58, 96
whale-watching 50, 59, 126, 127
Wi-Fi 124
Wildlife 50–51
Jökulsá á Dal 51
Jökulsárlón 32, 50
Lake Mývatn 50
Skjálfandi 50
Súðavík Arctic Fox Centre 90–1
watching 67
Þingvellir 13
see also Birds; Flora
Women travellers 123

Þ
Þingeyrakirkja 39, 98
Þingvallavatn 12, 108, 111
Þingvellir National Park 5, 10, **12–13**, 108, 111
hiking trails 54
itineraries 6, 85
Parliament site 67
Þjóðhátíð Vestmannaeyjar 68, 110
Þjóðminjasafn Íslands (National Museum) (Reykjavík) 40, 76, 77
Þjórsárdalur 109
Þorbjarnardóttir, Guðríður 37
Þórsmörk 55, 115
Þórsmörk Reserve 116

Acknowledgments

This edition updated by

Contributor Jenna Gottlieb
Senior Editor Alison McGill
Senior Designer Vinita Venugopal
Project Editors Dipika Dasgupta, Lucy Sara-Kelly
Project Art Editor Bharti Karakoti
Assistant Editor Anjasi N.N.
Picture Research Administrator Vagisha Pushp
Picture Research Manager Taiyaba Khatoon
Publishing Assistant Halima Mohammed
Jacket Designer Jordan Lambley
Senior Cartographer Subhashree Bharati
Cartography Manager Suresh Kumar
Senior DTP Designer Tanveer Zaidi
Senior Production Editor Jason Little
Production Controller Kariss Ainsworth
Deputy Managing Editor Beverly Smart
Managing Editors Shikha Kulkarni, Hollie Teague
Managing Art Editor Sarah Snelling
Senior Managing Art Editor Priyanka Thakur
Art Director Maxine Pedliham
Publishing Director Georgina Dee

DK would like to thank the following for their contribution to the previous editions: David Leffman, Michael Kissane, Bergljót Njóla Jakobsdóttir, Helen Peters, Nigel Hicks, Rough Guides/David Leffman.

Picture Credits

The publisher would like to thank the following for their kind permission to reproduce their photographs.
Key: a-above; b-below/bottom; c-centre; f-far; l-left; r-right; t-top

123RF.com: pitinan21br.

4Corners: SIME/Olimpio Fantuz 3tl, 72–3; SIM /Maurizio Rellini 56–7.

Alamy Stock Photo: Egill Bjarnason 64b; COMPAGNON Bruno 33br; PHOTOFVG RM COLLECTION 66crb; imageBROKER/Dr. Torsten Heydenreich 90b; Arctic Images 68bc; Joana Kruse 71br; Barry Lewis 62t; Icelandic photo agency 61br; Mary Evans Picture Library 36tl; Icelandic photo agency/Sigurdur Jokull Olafsson 60t; Graham Prentice 74tl; Steven Sheppardson 37t.

Ásgeir Helgi & Agust G. Atlason: 68b.

Corbis: Arctic-Images/SuperStock 70t; Arctic-Images 4b, 59tr, 52br, 116b; Hans Strand 115t.

Dreamstime.com: Sylvia Adams 32clb; Adreslebedev 4clb; Aiisha 4t, 24cl; Andreanita 24bl; Claudio Balducelli 20–21c; Gisli Baldursson 33tl, 51tr; Darius Baužys 13tl; Andrey Bayda 49tl; Bilderschorsch 104bl; Sigurdur William Brynjarsson 2tr, 34–5; Cadifor 103bc; Checco 50br, 54t; Demerzel21 2tl, 8–9, 106–107; Derwuth 76b; Filip Fuxa 7cr, 10bl, 46crb, 85bl; Gkoultouridis 16–7c; H368k742 59clb, 67tr; Jon Helgason 46tc; Humgate 7tr; Iaceo 6cl; Martín Zalba Ibanez 32br; Dmitry Islentyev 14bl; Jarcosa98crb; Javarman 30–31c; Jeremyreds 3tr, 118–19; Aagje De Jong 55cl; Þórarinn Jónsson 45b; Kreierson 12br; Oleksandr Korzhenko 84t; Ivan Kurmyshov 103cla; Thomas Langlands 27tl; Florence Mcginn 28–9c, minnystock 11t; Nur Ismail Mohammad 102b; Erzsi Molnár 51cl; Oriontrail 77cla; Parys 48bl; Pedja77 50clb; Tawatchai Prakobkit 66t; Johann Ragnarsson 49crb; Michael Ransburg 18–19c, 71tl; Arseniy Rogov 48tc; Sanspek 4cla; Selitbul 52br; Serinus 4cl; Rafn Sigurbjörnsson 11crb; Marteinn Sigurdsson 90cra; Smallredgirl 10cb; Kippy Spilker 13cb; Standret 22–3; Alexey Stiop 29cl; Takepicsforfun 4crb; Tatonka 96b; Ryan Taylor 10–11b; Milan_tesar 31bl; Alexey Tkachenko 60bc; Tomas1111 26cl, 39tl; Maksym Topchii 25tl; Larysa Uhryn 47b; Ucheema 4cra; Ukrphoto 63tr; Victorianl 11cra; Corepics Vof 30bl; Dennis Van De Water 14–5c; Wkruck 11c; Sara Winter 18br; Zbindere 89br.

Fishmarkadurinn: Bjorn Arnason 62br.

FLPA: Bill Coster 20b; ImageBroker 67br.

Getty Images: Bloomberg 37br; Corbis NX/Arctic-Images 58bl; Patrick Dieudonne 86tc; Michele Falzone 42tr; Atli Mar Hafsteinsson 86bl; Thorsten Henn 53cl; Lonely Planet Images 6tr; Richard Manin 42bl; Martin Moos 88tl.

Grái Kötturinn: 80bl.

Hótel Geysir: 17tl.

Inside the Volcano: Sølve Fredheim 112bl.

iStockphoto.com: Olga_Gavrilova 16clb, parys 21tl, E+ / SimonSkafar 1.

Kirsuberjatréð: 79tr.

National Museum of Iceland, ÞJÓÐMINJASAFN ÍSLANDS: 40cl.

Nielsen Restaurant: 105tr.

Photoshot: Stefan Auth 94tl; Picture Alliance/Carsten Schmidt 24br.

Rauða Húsið: 113tr.

Rex Features: Agencia EFE 69tr.

Reykjavík City Museum: G. Bjarki Gudmundsson 41br.

Sjavargrillid: 81cr

Sigurjón Ólafsson Museum: Embrace-NATO, 1949, by Sigurjón Ólafsson LSÓ 1 41tl.

Þrír Frakkar: Picasa 65cr.

Cover

Front and spine: **iStockphoto.com:** E+ / SimonSkafar.

Back: **Dreamstime.com:** ristinn Kristinsson tr, **Getty Images:** Moment / Somnuk Krobkum crb; **iStockphoto.com:** E+ / SimonSkafar b; David Watts Jr. tl; **Getty Images:** L. Toshio Kishiyama cla.

Pull out map cover

iStockphoto.com: E+ / SimonSkafar.

All other images © Dorling Kindersley
For further information see: www.dkimages.com

Penguin Random House

First edition 2010

Published in Great Britain by Dorling Kindersley Limited DK, One Embassy Gardens, 8 Viaduct Gardens, London SW11 7BW, UK

The authorised representative in the EEA is Dorling Kindersley Verlag GmbH. Arnulfstr. 124, 80636 Munich, Germany

Published in the United States by DK Publishing, 1745 Broadway, 20th Floor, New York, NY 10019, USA

Copyright © 2010, 2023 Dorling Kindersley Limited A Penguin Random House Company

23 24 25 26 10 9 8 7 6 5 4 3 2 1

The publishers cannot accept responsibility for any consequences arising from the use of this book, nor for any material on third party websites, and cannot guarantee that any website address in this book will be a suitable source of travel information.

A CIP catalogue record is available from the British Library.

A catalogue record for this book is available from the Library of Congress.

ISSN 1479-344X
ISBN 978-0-2416-1592-8

Printed and bound in Malaysia

www.dk.com

As a guide to abbreviations in visitor information blocks: **Adm** = admission charge; **D** = dinner; **L** = lunch.

Phrase Book

Icelandic is a Nordic language. Many of its sounds do not exist in English, so the pronunciations below are for guidance only. Icelandic has three letters that do not exist in modern English: þ ("thorn", pronounced as th as in "thin"); ð ("eth", pronounced as soft th as in "the"); æ ("aye", pronounced as i as in "light"). Stress falls on the first syllable of the word.

Guidelines for Pronunciation

Vowels

There are seven vowels – a, e, i, o, u, y and æ, five of which take a stress accent, which changes the pronunciation. The "o" can have an umlaut over it.

a = as in "sat"	*á* = ow as in "owl"
e = as in "met"	*i* = as in "sit"
í = ee as in "feel"	*o* = as in "hot"
ó = as in "hole"	*ö* = "uh" sound
u = as in "put"	*ú* = oo as in "fool"
ý = ee as in "meet"	*æ* = i as in "light"

Letter combinations

Some combined letters in Icelandic have special pronunciations.

au = as o in "hole"	*ei* = as ai in "hail"
ey = as ai in "hail"	*fn* = as bn
ll = as tl	*sj* = as sh in "fish"
fl = as bl, but as fl at the start of a word	
ng = as nk at the end of a word, as ng in the middle	

In an Emergency

Help!	**Hjálp!**	*hy-oulp*
Call a doctor	**Náið í lækni**	*nou-ith ee laek-ni*
Call an ambulance	**Hringdu í sjúkrabíl**	*hreen-du ee syoo-kra-beel*
Call the police	**Hringdu í lögregluna**	*hreen-du ee leu-rekl-una*
Call the fire brigade	**Hringdu í slökkviliðið**	*hreen-du ee sleuk-vi-lith-ith*

Communication Essentials

Yes	**Já**	*yow*
No	**Nei**	*nay*
Please (offering)	**Gjörðu svo vel**	*gyeurth-u svo vel*
Thank you	**Takk/takk fyrir**	*takk /takk fir-ir*
Excuse me	**Afsakið**	*af-sak-ith*
Hello	**Halló**	*hallo*
Hello (polite)	**Vertu sæll/sæll**	*vert-u sael(f.)/saetl(m.)*
Goodbye	**Bless**	*bless*
Good night /morning /evening	**Góða nótt /morgunn Gott kvöld**	*go-tha nott go-tha morg-un gott kveu-ld*

Useful Phrases

How are you?	**Hvað segirðu gott?**	*kvahth say-irth-u gott*
Very well, thank you.	**Allt gott**	*alht gott*
That's fine.	**Það er fínt/ gott**	*thath er feen-t/ gott*
Where is/ are ...?	**Hvar er/ eru ...?**	*kvar er/ eru*
How do I get to ...?	**Hvernig kemst ég til ...?**	*kvern-ig kem-st yieg til*

Do you speak English?	**Talarðu ensku?**	*tal-arth-u ensk-u*
I don't understand.	**Ég skil ekki**	*yieg skil ekki*

Shopping

How much does this cost?	**Hvað kostar þetta?**	*kvath kost-ar thett-a*
I would like ...	**Ég ætla að fá ...**	*yieg aetla ath fou*
Do you take ... credit cards? traveller's cheques?	**Takið þið ... kreditkort? ferðatékka?**	*tak-ith thith kre-dit-kort ferth-a-tiekk-a*
What time do you open/ close?	**Hvenær opnið þið/ lokið þið?**	*kven-aer oph-nith thith/ lok-ith thith*
this one	**þessi hérna**	*thessi hier-nah*
that one	**þessi þarna**	*thessi thar-nah*
expensive	**dýrt**	*deer-t*
size	**stærð**	*sdaerth*

Types of Shop

bakery	**bakarí**	*ba-ka-ree*
bank	**banki**	*boun-ki*
chemist	**apótek**	*ap-o-tek*
fishmonger	**fiskibúð**	*fisk-i-booth*
garage (mechanics)	**bílaverkstæði**	*beel-a-verk-staeth-i*
market	**markaður**	*mark-ath-ur*
post office	**pósthús**	*post-hoos*
supermarket	**matarverslun**	*mah-dar-vers-lun*
travel agent	**ferðaskrifstofa**	*ferta-skrif-sdofa*

Sightseeing

art gallery	**listagallerí**	*list-ah-gall-er-ee*
bay	**flói**	*flo-i*
beach	**fjara**	*fyar-ah*
bike	**reiðhjól**	*raith-hyeeol*
bus (town)	**strætó**	*straeh-tou*
bus (long dist.)	**rúta**	*roo-ta*
bus station	**umferðami-ðstöð**	*um-fertha-mith-steuth*
bus ticket	**strætó/rútu miði**	*straeh-tou/roo-tu mithi*
car	**bíll**	*bee-dlh*
car rental	**bílaleiga**	*bee-la-laig-a*
cathedral	**dómkirkja**	*dom-kirk-ya*
church	**kirkja**	*kirk-ya*
glacier	**jökull**	*yeu-kudl*
harbour	**höfn**	*heubn*
hot spring	**hver**	*kver*
island	**eyja**	*ai-yah*
lake	**stöðuvatn**	*steu-thu-vatn*
mountain	**fjall**	*fyadlh*
museum	**safn**	*sabn*
tourist information	**upplýsinga-miðstöð**	*uph-lees-eenga-mith-sdeuth*
waterfall	**foss**	*foss*

Staying in a Hotel

Do you have a vacant room?	**Eigið þið laust herbergi?**	*aigith thith laost her-berg-i*
double room with double bed	**Tveggja manna herbergi með hjónarúmi**	*tvegg-ya mann-a her-berg-i meth hyonah-roommi*
twin room	**tveggja manna herbergi**	*tvegg-ya mann-a her-berg-i*

single room	**eins manns herbergi**	*ayns manns her-berg-i*
room with bath/shower	**herbergi með baði/sturtu**	*her-berg-i meth bath-i/sturh-ta*
I have a reservation	**Ég á pantað**	*yieg ou pant-ath*

Eating Out

Have you got a table?	**Eigið þið laust borð?**	*aigith thith laost borth*
I'd like to reserve a table.	**Gæti ég pantað borð.**	*gyaet-i yieg pant-ath borth*
breakfast	**morgunmatur**	*morg-un-mat-ur*
lunch	**hádegismatur**	*hou-deg-is-mat-ur*
dinner	**kvöldmatur**	*kveuld-mat-ur*
The bill, please.	**Reikninginn takk.**	*raikn-ing-inn takk*
waitress/waiter	**þjónn**	*thyo-dn*
menu	**matseðill**	*maht-seth-idl*
starter	**smáréttur**	*smou-riet-ur*
first course	**forréttur**	*for-riet-ur*
main course	**aðalréttur**	*athal-riet-ur*
dessert	**eftirréttur**	*eft-ir-riet-ur*
wine list	**vínlisti**	*veen-list-i*
glass	**glas**	*glas*
bottle	**flaska**	*flask-a*
knife	**hnífur**	*hneev-ur*
fork	**gaffall**	*gaff-adl*
spoon	**skeið**	*skaith*

Menu Decoder

bjór	*byorh*	beer
brauð	*braoth*	bread
ferskir ávextir	*fersk-ir ou-vekst-irh*	fresh fruit
fiskur	*fisk-ur*	fish
franskar	*fransk-ar*	chips
grænmeti	*graen-met-i*	vegetables
grillað	*grill-ath*	grilled
gufusoðið	*gu-vu-soth-ith*	poached
hvítvín	*kveet-veen*	white wine
ís	*ees*	ice cream
kaka/ vínarbrauð	*ca-ka/ veen-ar-braoth*	cake/ pastry
kartöflur	*kart-eufl-ur*	potatoes
kjöt	*kyeut*	meat
kjúklingur	*kyook-leeng-ur*	chicken
lambakjöt	*lamb-ah-kyeut*	lamb
laukur	*laok-ur*	onions
lax	*laks*	salmon
mjólk	*myolk*	milk
nautasteik	*nao-ta-staik*	beef
ostur	*os-tur*	cheese
pipar	*phi-par*	pepper
pylsa/ pulsa	*pils-ah/ pul-sah*	hotdog
rauðvín	*raoth-veen*	red wine
rækjur	*rai-kyur*	prawns
sjávarréttur	*syou-va-rietd-ur*	seafood
smjör	*smyeurh*	butter
soðið	*soth-ith*	boiled
sódavatn	*so-da-vadn*	mineral water
sósa	*so-sa*	sauce
steikt	*staikt*	fried
súkkulaði	*sook-u-lath-i*	chocolate
súpa	*soo-ba*	soup
svínakjöt	*sveen-a-kyeut*	pork

sykur	*siik-ur*	sugar
te	*teh*	tea
vatn	*vahdn*	water
ýsa	*ee-sa*	haddock

Useful Signs

open	**opið**	*op-ith*
closed	**lokað**	*lohk-ath*
entry	**inn/inngangur**	*inn/inn-goung-ur*
exit	**út/útgangur**	*oot/oot-goung-ur*
jeep track	**jeppaslóð**	*yepp-ah-sloth*
parking	**bílastæði**	*bee-la-staeth-i*
one-lane bridge	**einbreið brú**	*ayn-braith broo*
danger	**hætta**	*haett-ah*
forbidden	**bannað**	*bann-ath*
end of tarmac	**malbik slitlag endar**	*mal-bik slit-lag end-ar*
campsite	**tjaldsvæði**	*tyald-svaeth-i*
toilet	**klósett**	*clo-sett*
ladies' toilet	**kvennaklósett**	*kvenn-a-clo-sett*
gents' toilet	**karlaklósett**	*karl-a-clo-sett*

Time

one minute	**ein mínúta**	*ayn meen-oot-a*
one hour	**ein klukkustund**	*ayn kluk-u-stun-dh*
a day	**dagur**	*dag-ur*
Monday	**mánudagur**	*moun-u-dag-ur*
Tuesday	**þriðjudagur**	*thrith-yu-dag-ur*
Wednesday	**miðvikudagur**	*mith-vik-u-dag-ur*
Thursday	**fimmtudagur**	*fimt-u-dag-ur*
Friday	**föstudagur**	*feust-u-dag-ur*
Saturday	**laugardagur**	*laog-ar-dag-ur*
Sunday	**sunnudagur**	*sunnu-dag-ur*

Numbers

1	**einn**	*aydn*
2	**tveir**	*tvayr*
3	**þrír**	*threer*
4	**fjórir**	*fyor-ir*
5	**fimm**	*fim*
6	**sex**	*segs*
7	**sjö**	*syeu*
8	**átta**	*outt-a*
9	**níu**	*nee-u*
10	**tíu**	*tee-u*
11	**ellefu**	*edl-ev-u*
12	**tólf**	*tolvh*
13	**þrettán**	*thrett-dyoun*
14	**fjórtán**	*fyorh-dyoun*
15	**fimmtán**	*fim-dyoun*
16	**sextán**	*segs-dyoun*
17	**sautján**	*sao-dyoun*
18	**átján**	*out-dyoun*
19	**nítján**	*nee-dyoun*
20	**tuttugu**	*tutt-ug-u*
21	**tuttugu og einn**	*tutt-ug-u og aydn*
30	**þrjátíu**	*thryou-tee-u*
40	**fjörtíu**	*fyeur-tee-u*
50	**fimmtíu**	*fim-tee-u*
60	**sextíu**	*segs-tee-u*
70	**sjötíu**	*syeu-tee-u*
80	**áttatíu**	*outt-a-tee-u*
90	**níutíu**	*nee-u-tee-u*
100	**hundrað**	*hund-rath*
1000	**þúsund**	*thoos-und*
1,000,000	**milljón**	*mil-ee-yon*

Iceland Town Index

Akranes	B5	Flateyri	B2	Hvammstangi	C3
Akureyri	E2	Flókalundur	B2	Hveragerði	C5
Bakkafjörður	G2	Flúðir	C5	Hvolsvöllur	C6
Bergþórshvoll	C6	Garður	B5	Keflavík	B5
Bifröst	C4	Gjögur	C2	Keldur	D5
Bíldudalur	A2	Grenivik	E2	Kirkjubæjarklaustur	E5
Blönduós	D2	Grímsstaðir	F2	Kópasker	F1
Bolungarvík	B1	Grindavík	B5	Krýsuvík	B5
Borðeyri	C3	Grund	E3	Laugar	C3
Borgarfjörður Eystri	H2	Grundarfjörður	B3	Laugarvatn	C5
Borgarnes	B4	Hafnarfjörður	B5	Miðsandur	C4
Breiðavík	A2	Hafnir	B5	Möðrudalur	F3
Breiðdalsvík	H4	Hallormsstaður	G3	Neskaupstaður	H3
Brjánslækur	B3	Haukadalur	C5	Norðurfjörður	C2
Brú	C3	Hella	C5	Ólafsfjörður	E2
Búðir	A4	Hellissandur	A3	Ólafsvík	A4
Dalvík	E2	Hellnar	A4	Patreksfjörður	A2
Djúpavík	C2	Hnjótur	A2	Raufarhöfn	F1
Djúpivogur	G4	Höfn	G5	Reyðarfjörður	G3
Dritvík	A4	Hofsós	D2	Reykhólar	B3
Egilsstaðir	G3	Hólar	D2	Reykholt	C4
Eiðar	G3	Hólmavík	C2	Reykjahlíð	F2
Eskifjörður	H3	Hrafnagil	E2	Reykjanes	B2
Eyrarbakki	C5	Hrafnseyri	B2	Reykjavík	B5
Fagurhólsmýri	F5	Húsafell	C4	Rif	A3
Fáskrúðsfjörður	H3	Húsavík	E2	Sandgerði	B5
Fellabær	G3	Hvallátur	A2	Sauðárkrókur	D2
Selárdalur	A2
Selatangar	B5
Selfoss	C5
Seyðisfjörður	G3
Siglufjörður	D2
Skaftafell	F5
Skagaströnd	C2
Skálholt	C5
Skógar	D6
Stöðvarfjörður	H4
Stokkseyri	C5
Stykkishólmur	B3
Súðavík	B2
Suðureyri	B2
Svalbarðseyri	E2
Tálknafjörður	A2
Vegamót	B4
Viðimýri	D3
Vík	D6
Vopnafjörður	G2
Þingeyrar	C2
Þingeyri	B2
Þorlákshöfn	C5
Þórshöfn	G1

Reykjavík Selected Street Index

Aðalstræti	K2	Fríkirkjuvegur	L3	Kringlumýrarbraut	Q3
Ægisgata	K2	Furumelur	J3	Kvisthagi	J3
Ánanaust	J1	Gamla Hringbraut	M4	Lækjargata	L2
Aragata	K4	Garðastræti	K2	Langahlíð	N4
Ásvallagata	J2	Geirsgata	K2	Laufásvegur	L4
Audarstræti	M4	Grandagarður	K1	Laugalækur	K4
Austurstræti	L2	Grandavegur	J2	Laugarnesvegur	Q2
Baldursgata	L3	Grenimelur	J3	Laugateigur	Q3
Bankastræti	L2	Grettisgata	M3	Leifsgata	M4
Barónsstígur	M4	Guðbrandsg	K3	Leirulækur	R2
Bárugata	K2	Guðrg	M4	Meistaravellir	J2
Bergstaðastræti	L3	Gunnarsbraut	M4	Miðtún	P3
Bergþórugata	M3	Háahlíð	N6	Miklabraut	N5
Birkimelur	K3	Hafnarstræti	L2	Mýrargata	K1
Blómvallag	K2	Hagamelur	J3	Njálsgata	M3
Bólstaðarhlíð	N5	Hagatorg	J3	Nóatún	P3
Borgartún	P3	Hamrahlíð	N6	Nýlendugata	K1
Bræðraborgarstígur	K2	Háteigsvegur	N4	Ránargata	K1
Bragagata	L3	Hátún	P3	Rauðarárstígur	N3
Brautarholt	P3	Hávallagata	K2	Reykjahlíð	N5
Brynjólfsgata	J4	Hellus	L3	Reynimelur	J3
Bústaðavegur	N6	Hjarðarhagi	J4	Sæbraut	R1
Dunhagi	J4	Höfðatún	N3	Sæmundargata	K4
Eggertsgata	K5	Hofsvallagata	J3	Seljavegur	J1
Egilsgata	M4	Holtsgata	J2	Sigtún	Q3
Eiríksgata	M4	Hörgshlíð	N6	Sjafnarg	L4
Engjavegur	R4	Hringbraut	L4	Skálhst	L3
Eskihlíð	N5	Hrísateigur	Q2	Skipholt	P4
Espimelur	J3	Hverfisgata	M3	Skógarhlíð	M5
Fiskislóð	K1	Ingólfsstræti	L2	Skólavörðustígur	L3
Fjólugata	L3	Kalkofnsv	L2	Skothúsvegur	K3
Flókagata	N4	Kaplaskjólsvegur	J2	Skúlagata	N3
Fornhagi	J4	Kirkjuteigur	Q3	Smáragata	L4
Frakkastígur	M3	Klapparstígur	M3	Snorrabraut	N3
Freyjugata	M4	Klettagarðar	R1	Sóleyjargata	L3
Sóltún	P3
Sólvallagata	J2
Sölvhólsg	M2
Stakkahlíð	N5
Stórholt	N4
Sturlugata	K4
Suðurgata	K4
Suðurlandsbraut	R2
Sundlaugarvegur	R2
Tjarnargata	K3
Tómasarhagi	J4
Tryggvagata	L2
Túngata	K2
Urðarst	L3
Vesturgata	K1
Vesturvallag	J2
Viðimelur	J3
Vitastígur	M3
Vonarstræti	L2
Þingholtsstræti	L3
Þverholt	N4